THE EMBEDDED ENTREPRENEUR

HOW TO BUILD AN AUDIENCE-DRIVEN BUSINESS

ARVID KAHL

THE BOOT
STRAPPED
FOUNDER

Links in this book are protected by PermanentLink (learn more at https://permanent.link).

Cover design by Yasir Farhan (dezinir.99).

Illustrations by Graeme Crawley.

ISBN: 978-3-9821957-6-6 (Paperback)

ISBN: 978-3-9821957-7-3 (Hardcover)

ISBN: 978-3-9821957-8-0 (eBook)

ISBN: 978-3-9821957-9-7 (ePDF)

Version 1.0.4 (May 11th, 2021)

For my grandma Brigitta.

Thank you for teaching me empathy and how to listen.
I learned what service is from how you served those around you.

Most of life is a search for who and what needs you the most.

NAVAL RAVIKANT

CONTENTS

INTRODUCTION

This is not an idea book. This is a book for people who need actionable advice.

Instead of trying to convince you to build an audience, let me share the stories of those who have done it well and then equip you with the tools and strategies to build an audience-driven business.

You will learn how to discover your future audience, how to embed yourself in your audience's communities, how to extract business opportunities through observation, and how to build a following that will grow your personal and professional brand.

Here is some inspiration.

When Paul Jarvis had the idea for a simple and privacy-focused analytics software, he tweeted a mockup image of the product to his Twitter audience. While the tweet has since been deleted, here is what it contained:

What if website analytics software didn't take your users data to line their pockets from advertising? What is website analytics software was simple and trustworthy? Here's my new idea (and if this gets enough traction, I'll build it) https://usefathom.com/

Funny how the initial mockup isn't *that* far off from our current version in terms of its goal.

That initial sketch got retweeted over 500 times, which gave him the confidence to start his journey building Fathom Analytics[1], which grew into a successful alternative to much more prominent players in the space. Paul and his co-founder Jack Ellis focus on building only features that benefit the majority of their customers. They make sure their vision of a privacy-first product reflects the needs and priorities of their audience.

Rosie Sherry was a software tester, ensuring that freshly created software products were delivering what they promised. Rosie co-founded a software testing agency. She was part of the software testing community. Looking at how engineers and marketers had all those fancy conferences and communities to learn from, Rosie felt that her fellow testers didn't get the same level of attention. She listened to what her community members needed and created a testing-centric community with The Ministry of Testing, organizing multiple conferences every year into a multi-million-dollar business. Rosie became an expert in both testing and community-building, which led her to build Rosieland, a community for community-builders.

After Slack acquired and shut down the popular screen-sharing software ScreenHero, an outcry went through the software engineering community. Ben Orenstein was there to listen. He knew exactly why people mourned the loss of that particular feature: he'd been doing pair programming that way for years. Ben and his co-founders started working on the remote pair programming product Tuple to allow engineers to continue working together as they had done in the past. Since then, Tuple has grown into a successful and sustainable Software-as-a-Service (SaaS) business.

A common thread between these founders is their dedication to their audience. They put their audiences first: they listened to the people in communities they were members of, found problems they were excited to solve, and built a following while creating successful services and products. Instead of assuming they knew exactly what their future customers would need, they put their audience first, at all times. Whenever it came to a decision, they gathered feedback from their audiences — their peers — and ensured that the results would benefit their growing following of customers, prospects, and supporters. Paul, Rosie, and Ben are Embedded Entrepreneurs.

The working title for this book was "Audience First." You might have heard that term before. Quite likely, someone explained it as "build a following on social media, then sell them something." To me, this is too narrow a definition of something that could be so much more. I believe "audience-first" starts long before you build an audience: from being part of a community to observing, interacting, and being embedded among the people you want to serve, there are many things to do before you start building a following.

In fact, this focus on people, where they congregate, and what they need deserves a better name altogether. I call it the "Audience-Driven approach" to building a business. A lot of this process takes place inside of communities; as places of exchange, learning, and teaching, they allow their members to build a reputation as valued contributors.

A community can be an audience eventually.

At first, communities are hunting grounds for great opportunities, then they turn into places to build meaningful relationships, and later they'll be the fertile soil in which you will grow your business. At all points, the community members are a potential audience for what you have to say and what you offer.

Focusing on your audience from day one has several advantages over the common product-first strategy, where founders come up with a product idea before they do any market research or audience discovery. Founders that go "idea-first" often build businesses that are "solutions looking for a problem." The "idea-first" approach results in products that are lacking validation and are built without a clear audience in mind.

The Audience-Driven approach turns all these uncertainties into advantages:

- **Validation is built-in:** you're constantly interacting with the people you want to serve and empower, which leads to much faster feedback loops. You get to experience their problems first-hand, you have access to real people with real struggles, and you can collaborate with your audience to build a solution that works for them.
- **You aren't leaving much to chance:** you know that there are real people out there feeling a painful

problem, and you can check if they are already spending money attempting to solve it, thus increasing your chances of building something people are willing to pay for.

- **You create a personal brand that transcends the business you're currently working on:** even if your startup fails, you continue to be a domain expert in that field.

This is the path of the Embedded Entrepreneur. This book will expand the meaning and the process of building an audience-driven business into a full strategy for creating an abundance of value while paving the way to your financial independence.

This book will help you with actionable guidance on your entrepreneurial journey.

If you're an aspiring entrepreneur, you should read this book cover to cover. The chapters are mostly self-contained, and you can skip any amount of chapters depending on your immediate needs. But beware: too many entrepreneurs have thought they didn't need to learn more about their audience before building their product and ultimately have failed. If you want to make sure you validate your business efforts from day one, try resisting the urge to skip to a later chapter. Your future self will thank you.

If you have just decided to become an entrepreneur and are looking for the right starting point for your business, start with the **Audience-Driven Movement** part of the book. This will be the foundation for all your entrepreneurial efforts and is the most critical step to get right.

For founders who want to dive right into discovering an audience to serve, you'll find the **Audience Discovery** section helpful.

If you already know who you're going to serve, you can jump to the **Audience Exploration** part of the book.

If you are very sure that you are suitably embedded into your audience's community but you're not sure which problem is the right one to solve, head over to the **Problem Discovery** section.

Finally, if you already are working on a validated solution to an equally validated problem and want to skip to the audience-building part immediately, start your reading journey at the **Audience-Building** part of the book.

Wherever you start, I hope you find the tools and motivation to start building (for) your very own audience. Let's get started!

THE AUDIENCE-DRIVEN
MOVEMENT

An audience used to be a group of people in front of a stage. The band would play their songs, and the audience would cheer. The lead singer would yell something at them, and the audience would applaud. The only person with something to say would be the rock star. You couldn't distinguish any other single voice from all the yelling and shouting. An audience was a one-way-street.

Times have changed.

In a globally connected world full of creators, it's not enough to *talk at* people anymore. Today, successful entrepreneurs *talk with* their audience; they engage with them on a level that the business world has never seen before.

Today, *everyone* is on stage.

Founders understand that an audience is not a mere distribution channel but a fundamental component of their business's success.

The Audience-Driven approach is about making every business choice with your audience in mind, including what to offer in the first place. Conducting business becomes a conversation, a consistent back-and-forth between entrepreneur and prospective customers. This conversation never ends. Even when the business succeeds beyond the founder's wildest dreams, the exchange with their audience's needs and desires continues. An audience is not a group of voiceless consumers. They are real people, and they expect to be treated accordingly by the founders and employees of a business.

A great example of this is Patrick Collison, CEO and co-founder of Stripe, a billion-dollar payments company. Patrick publicly asked[1] his customers to suggest items for Stripe's roadmap and engaged with hundreds of replies to that tweet. He was in touch with his customers in the early days when the business was named /dev/payments, and he is still in touch with them today. Of course, Stripe has internal teams prioritizing and implementing features. But they also listen to their developer audience, even though they are worth billions. This is what relentlessly focusing on your audience looks like.

Audience-First

I want to make sure that the terms and definitions I use in this book are precise. The term "audience-first" is commonly understood in a way that I find much too restrictive. Audience-first is short-hand for "build an audience first," the practice of building a large online following before selling them the products you create. While this is definitely a part of being "audience-driven," it's just one part of many.

What I want to focus on is a different way of involving your audience. I want to talk about a more immersive, "Audience-Driven" approach to business. Instead of just building a following, I want to focus on "putting the audience first," the public practice of engaging and interacting with the people you have chosen to empower from the very start. Don't worry: audience-building will play a significant part in this, but it's not the first step in the process of building (for) an audience; it's actually the final step.

Audience

That brings me to the term "audience."

An audience is everyone who should be interested in you, your business, and your products.

They are not just walking wallets. An audience is a group of real people with desires, dreams, and problems. If you want to build an audience-first business, you will need to build honest and authentic relationships with actual human beings.

Your audience doesn't have to exist yet for you to understand who they could be. Members of all kinds of communities could be part of your audience eventually. There are many potential future audience members out there, and it's your task to find them.

Community

An audience is not the same as a community, but they are related. Communities are focal points of audiences and a big part of the day-to-day work of the Embedded Entrepreneur. However, audiences extend way beyond individual communities. They span a multitude of communities, from virtual places to the real world. Communities are great resources and excellent starting points. However, an audience is needed to drive your business.

A community looks in all kinds of directions, but an audience looks at you.

In a community, people show up because of each other and what they create together. In an audience, they show up because of you and what you create.

The Audience-Driven Approach

The Audience-Driven approach's core principle is simple: you delay defining "the idea" and your product until after you have chosen and explored an audience for your business — because you can't know what your future customers need without understanding them first. You first choose a market to operate in, find a potential audience to serve, embed yourself within their communities, and learn what you need to create to solve their critical problems. Then, and only then, do you work on your idea — and create a following along the way.

An Audience-Driven approach removes the assumption that you know what your product will be before engaging your customers. It also makes customer and product development easier to accomplish by building validation and feedback loops into the discovery process from day one. That makes it something that can be done as a side project or without much capital commitment. With less guesswork and fewer wasted resources, this otherwise cumbersome process becomes something swift and attainable for bootstrapped and customer-funded businesses.

If you can't rely on millions in venture funding, you'll need to play it safe. Focusing on your audience will allow you to reduce the odds of failing by validating every step along the way. At the same time, the chances of having to make a full pivot — changing your whole business from target audience to which product you sell — become much lower.

The Product-First Approach

If the Audience-Driven approach lowers these risks, which alternative process has the highest risk of failure? That would be the product-first approach: the concept of coming up with a "really good idea" and assuming that you'll be able to figure out who you can sell it to at some later point. This is particularly dangerous now that more and more businesses are bootstrapped.

Why do so many founders go product-first and fail? Why is there such an avalanche of products being launched on ProductHunt every single day, only to vanish into obscurity?

I call this the "entrepreneurial curse": we founders assume too much. At its very core, we need to assume that things will work out fine to find the motivation to start a business. That's the healthy part. But we then take it too far. We assume that we know our market, who our audience is, and what they need. First, we create a concept, then develop something, test it briefly, and finally launch the product, expecting it to "just work" from the start. "Build it and they will come." This approach is very risky. Few startups know their markets or even themselves.

It's the natural instinct of an entrepreneur to think that they know what product they will eventually deliver. We are surrounded by products every minute of our day. Everything we touch and use to go through our lives is a solution to some problem. We're focused on seeing solutions and often neglect to visualize the underlying problems. So when we have a business idea, the solutions we envision are usually much clearer to us than the problems they are supposed to solve — or if there are enough people who feel this problem strongly enough to consider paying for a solution.

Often, it's not even clear if the problem that the product solves actually exists. The proverbial "Tinder for Cats" is an example of a solution to a non-existent problem. It might be a fun project to try out a new app development framework, but it won't result in a product that you can run a business around.

In reality, "solutions looking for a problem" are much more subtle.

Every day, a developer somewhere considers building another variation of an existing tool. They build this because they need it themselves, but they don't consider if their need is a commonly shared one. Many first-time entrepreneurs consider their problem perception and how they approach solving their issue to be the truth for all other people in their industry. They focus solely on building, and then they try to find a market for their product[2].

But this is self-delusion: it's building upon unvalidated assumptions. Product-first founders "get out of the building" too late. They talk to their customers — if they can even find any — after they have developed their product and then try to convince them that they should buy it. That takes time, it takes money, and it is an overall stressful activity. The Audience-Driven approach takes this further: instead of merely leaving the building to observe your prospects, you will learn how to embed yourself in their communities, build a reputation as a valued contributor, and build a business by solving their problems with and for them.

So, how can the Audience-Driven movement help you? Here

is a quick rundown of the approach that I will introduce in this book:

- **Audience Discovery:** Find your audience. The most important choice is who you want to serve. Deliberately selecting an audience is the foundation of a successful business. I will show you a tested and actionable five-step process to find the audience you want to empower.
- **Audience Exploration & Problem Discovery:** Understand the path. Building a business the audience-driven way requires you to be an active part of communities, which involves talking to people and learning from them. I will share strategies and tactics for how you can do this as effectively as possible.
- **Audience-Building:** Create (for) your audience. Working with and for your audience will allow you to build a product and a business that solves real problems for real people. By consistently showing up and providing value, you will become an expert that your audience will gladly follow. I will share the stories and approaches of the founders who have succeeded — and failed — to build their audience and businesses in public.

To start your journey to becoming an Embedded Entrepreneur, a founder who puts their audience first, you will need first to discover who you want to serve.

AUDIENCE DISCOVERY

AN ACTIONABLE GUIDE TO FINDING YOUR AUDIENCE

> " There are many fish in the sea, but never let a good one swim away.

MATSHONA DHLIWAYO

Let me introduce you to a data-driven method of finding a potential audience for your side business. It will allow you to discover an audience that will sustain a business for many years and make it an enjoyable journey.

Before we get to the step-by-step guide, I would like to address one particular problem that many newly minted entrepreneurs have, particularly when they come from an engineering background: they severely underestimate an audience's importance — with devastating consequences.

Have you ever been to a museum only to be shoved through a gift shop on your way out? The gift shops are not the main attraction, yet they contribute significantly to those institutions' bottom lines[1]. But no entrepreneur in their right mind would open a museum gift shop in their garage and expect it to make a profit.

A store stocked with art prints and interior design books needs a particular audience. Museums have understood that to sell art-related books to people, they need to put the store where their artsy audience already is: on their way out of an exhibition.

Museums have understood a core rule of a successful business: find your audience first, then sell them something they need. They think "audience-driven."

If museums have understood that, why do we still see so many founders creating solutions searching for a problem? Why do so many entrepreneurs strain their minds to find a "good business idea," jump to building the product, and then wonder why they can't seem to find anyone to buy their solution? And how can you avoid making this exact same mistake while building your own business?

It starts with the cure to all bias: introspection. Mainly, if you're coming from an engineering background, your perspective will be biased towards creating products. For makers, *everything* is a potential product. No matter if we are engineers, marketers, or product managers, we are trained to create products; we're trained to think product-first. We use products, we make products, and we know products.

Very often, we're also afraid to talk to people. We fear being ridiculed, ignored, or laughed at. Our ideas are still forming in our minds, and we're afraid that if we share them too early, people will trample on those precious seeds. We come up with all kinds of stories about why we know what people would say and think.

Sadly, that combination of product-focus and fear of external validation often leads us to a logical fallacy: we assume that since *we* felt the need for a specific thing to exist, *others* will have the same need. We wanted it, that must mean others will want it, too. And even when it's clear they don't, we push ourselves to think that someone will buy what we offer if we just sell it hard enough.

This approach is putting the cart before the horse. It's the wrong way around. If we build our product first and then ask who might want to buy it, we're leaving a lot to chance. It is like the infamous developer trope of testing things in production. You want to check if your code is working well before you deploy it to your customers. Why not do the same for your business?

The best way to keep the amount of guesswork to a minimum is a *"multi-stage validation"* approach. Instead of starting with an idea, spending a lot of time building a product, and *only then* checking if this solves a problem for someone out there, I recommend the following steps (each of which we'll dive into in more detail later).

1. First, *explore which audiences you want to help.* Select the audience you think is most likely to support your business endeavors. Validate: Make sure the audience is interesting for you, is the right size, has exciting problems, and is willing to pay for a solution.
2. Then, observe that audience and *detect their most critical problems.* Select the most critical problem among them. Validate: Ensure the problem is genuinely critical, people are already looking for solutions, and it can't be easily ignored or delegated.
3. Then, *envision a solution that solves this problem* within your audience's workflow. Validate: Make sure that your solution doesn't have unintended side-effects and solves their problem without adding additional work.
4. Finally, and only now, *think of the product.* In which medium do you need to provide your solution? Will it be a mobile app? A SaaS application? A platform? Or

will it have to be a technical solution at all? Now is the time for the "idea" and the "product."

If you follow these steps, you will notice that your "idea" has to wait. It's not a stroke of genius that comes out of nowhere, but rather a carefully deliberated consequence of three distinct validation steps. It would be best if you learned first who is out there, what struggles they genuinely have, and how you can best help them. This way, your product's chances of success are much higher than if you go with a completely unvalidated "idea."

The goal of this process is to help you find that initial audience. Let's start with exploring which audience fits you best and make sure it can support a business. In my mentoring work, I have discovered a five-step approach that produces remarkable results. It will allow you to find an audience that you can serve for a long time — and that will *serve you* for equally as long.

I will suggest pragmatic steps you can take to find your optimal audience. Find what works for you, and use this as the foundation of your own personal framework to tackle these problems. This five-step approach will give you data: numbers that you can inspect, weigh, and draw conclusions from.

The result of this exercise will be a list of audiences that you can help by building a product that solves their critical problem, resulting in the opportunity of building a sustainable business. It will be a ranked list, with the most likely candidate audiences at the top and less interesting ones at the bottom.

You'll need to take notes during the process. Either grab a pen and a few sheets of paper or fire up a note-taking app. We're going to create a table with a few dozen rows and several columns. Start with an empty spreadsheet, putting "Audience Name" in the first column.

Aa Audience Name

Setting the stage for audience discovery.

STEP 1: AWARENESS — THINK OF POSSIBLE AUDIENCES

To find a niche audience that will allow you to build a great business, you will first need to become aware of it. Some niches are clearly visible, and some are somewhat hidden. This step is concerned with finding them.

The goal of this step is to find a group of people you want to help. It should be a well-defined group, best centered around a common interest or activity. If you can't easily find communities for this group, don't worry. The important thing at this stage is that you are aware of who they are and what they are about.

An existing tribe will work best. Tribes consist of people who share an interest, are highly interconnected, and follow the same leaders. They make for wonderful niche audiences. You might be part of quite a few tribes at this very moment. Seth Godin uses a wonderful definition for tribes: "People like us do things like this."

Start with yourself, then expand from your inner circle towards the outer boundaries of the people you know.

Ask yourself:

- **What tribes do you belong to?** What communities are you part of, consciously (because you participate, like being a chess club member) and unconsciously (by affiliation, like being a sports fan)? It can involve virtual communities and real-world groups alike.
- **What hobbies do you have?** What do you enjoy enough to spend money on, even though it's not essential? Examples here are things like craft beer or fixing old cars. Find activities you have a budget for.
- **What has been your lifestyle in the past?** How did you find things to do every weekend back when you were in college or just starting out working? What groups did you hang out with then, and what was it that they found exciting to do? Can you reconnect with those groups?
- **What professions do you have?** What kinds of jobs have you been doing throughout your life? What types of professional communities have you been part of?
- **What companies do you work for?** Which companies are you a customer of? Think of all the different businesses you interact with and mentally categorize them into the groups they belong to.
- **What is your significant other doing?** What groups do they belong to that are different from your groups? What groups did they belong to before you met? When they were kids, what clubs and associations were they part of?
- **What groups do your parents and siblings belong to?** What jobs are they working in, what groups do they hang out with for fun? What are the things you talk about at family gatherings, about which they have surprising levels of insight?
- **What are the social circles you frequent?** What

kinds of people do you interact with? Think of a party, meetup, or gathering you've been to recently. Who are the types of people you click with most, and what do they do?

- Reflect on your past experiences, even if they are not as recent as a few years ago. You might want to revisit old movies, books, or videos from that time period, too. Just remember: the aim here is to reflect on who's been a meaningful part of your life so far and how they relate to one another.

After some reflection, try to figure out what kinds of groups people in these tribes have in common. You might be part of several tribes that overlap, and you might want to include some that are far from your current tribe but still related.

The list you came up with from this exercise should contain a few dozen audiences. Let me give you an example of what my personal list would look like:

Aa Audience Name

Software Engineers

Bootstrapped Founders

Non-fiction Authors

Science-Fiction Fans

Craft Beer Enthusiasts

Plumbers & Pipefitters

Nurses

Coffee Aficionados

Book Hoarders

Miniature Painters

Progressive Metal Fans

Lawyers & Notaries

Aquarium Owners

Opera Singers

Heavy Twitter Users

For each audience on this list, I either am an expert or have direct access to an expert in my friends and family circle. The full list I have collected over the last few years contains at least 300 different audiences. I bet you can come up with at least 100 distinct groups of people within a few hours.

Exploring Your Surroundings

Another way of finding audiences that you might not already be aware of is by looking at the things around you. For every object you see, think about 1) *who* made it, 2) *how* they made it, 3) who it is *for*, and 4) how they *use* it. While 1 and 4 give you audiences immediately, 2 and 3 allow you to think about the interactions that the object went through either while it was being made (think of all the many businesses and activities involved in the production chain of something like a sheet of paper: forestry, logging, paper mills, distribution, sales, marketing) or while it is being used (let's stick with paper: pen makers, printer factories, publishers, editors, book club organizers, wedding table card printers). Most objects, when examined like that, will bring to mind a few dozen audiences.

Niches vs. Worldviews

Amy Hoy of Stacking the Bricks stresses focusing on the opinions held within certain groups of people[1]. Niches define people by external factors, while worldviews are identity-related and internal. Rallying people around a cause they resonate with is a way to build a following and a business, particularly in underserved industries. During your search for potential audiences, reflect on the issues you feel strongly about, and consider who else might be interested in that.

You will be done with this step when you have a few dozen audiences, though it is best to aim to identify a hundred or more audiences. You're trying to find so many to open up your mind about what different things people do and congregate around. It's essential to step out of your comfort zone and expand the horizon of what you can work with. The real impact of transferable skills lies where they have not yet been transferred to. You are trying to find those places here.

Don't worry about having "too many options." While the paradox of choice — the more options we have, the harder it is to choose — is a very real phenomenon, the whole point of this exercise is to come up with as many audience candidates as possible and then filter them down in the later steps until only a handful of great options remain.

STEP 2: AFFINITY — FIND OUT HOW MUCH YOU CARE ABOUT THEM

With a list of possible audiences and niches, you now need to weed out the markets you don't care about enough.

Personally, I know I could build great software products for the tax industry, but I don't enjoy that particular field. They're an interesting audience with a budget, for sure, but I know that I'd quickly tire of implementing yet another change required by newly introduced regulation. It's just not for me.

No business was ever successfully built by a founder who didn't care about the people they were selling their product to. You need to feel the desire to help your customers genuinely, or you will lose interest in providing value to them at some point.

This is a very subjective step in the process. You will need to think for a few minutes about the kinds of people you expect to work with in each industry. This is best done by asking yourself a few questions listed below for each audience and giving every audience a score.

Add a new column to your spreadsheet, called "Affinity." For every row in your spreadsheet, you will need to produce a rating between 0 and 5. Zero means that you don't care about serving this audience at all, and 5 means that you want to devote your life to serving the people in that niche.

To find out how much affinity you have for an audience, ask yourself these questions, and quickly note down a 0–5 rating for each.

- Do you believe that the members of this audience deserve to succeed much more than they currently do?
- Do you imagine conversations with these people to be interesting, fruitful, and enjoyable?
- Do you see a more profound reason, a passion that drives this audience's members to do what they do?
- Is the audience doing something meaningful?
- Could the people in this niche be doing something more substantial?
- Do you think you would benefit from learning a lot about the work in this niche?

When you have answered all these questions, add up the point values you gave and divide them by the number of questions you asked yourself to find the average. This number is an indicator of how much you care about the audience.

Once you have done this, sort your list by the affinity average, descending. That view alone is often eye-opening, as you will see clusters appear. There will be a cluster of things you care about because you are part of those audiences. That's a great source of potential businesses, as you will be solving your own problems. Another exciting cluster is the group of audiences that you are genuinely interested in because a particular passion or a mission drives them. Here, you will find eager audience members willing to try out anything that makes their job easier because they believe it's an important job to do.

Aa Audience Name	# Affinity
Software Engineers	4
Bootstrapped Founders	5
Non-fiction Authors	5
Science-Fiction Fans	4
Craft Beer Enthusiasts	3
Plumbers & Pipefitters	1
Nurses	2
Coffee Aficionados	2
Book Hoarders	3
Miniature Painters	3
Progressive Metal Fans	3
Lawyers & Notaries	1
Aquarium Owners	2
Opera Singers	2
Heavy Twitter Users	5

This step will allow you to see quite clearly who you care about most.

Beware of prejudices at this stage. I suggest having a chat with a "resident expert" for each niche to get a feeling for the audience from the inside. Only then should you step through the questions.

Move the audiences with an affinity of 2 or less to another sheet of your spreadsheet. They're not prime targets for now, but you might change your mind later. We're interested only in audiences you care about at this point, as this will be a requirement for spending significant time and effort on the exploration and validation that follow now.

STEP 3: OPPORTUNITY — FIND OUT IF THEY HAVE INTERESTING PROBLEMS

With a trimmed-down list, you're ready for the next step. For each audience, you will want to find out if they have any interesting problems. You're not looking into finding their critical problem just yet, as you will only take a cursory view into your audience at this point, but be on the lookout nonetheless. If you see something that they really need help with, that's a good sign.

For each audience, do the following things to find out if they have problems that might interest you.

- **Find a few SaaS products in their space and see what problems they solve.** Are these genuinely exciting problems? Does solving these problems make a difference in a good way? If you're looking into helping coffee lovers, head over to ProductHunt and search for "Coffee Subscriptions" to see what kinds of existing solutions have had some prior success.
- **Find a community forum or social media group where your niche audience hangs out and go through their recent posts.** Are people struggling with things that you would find interesting to help

them with? Do you think the audience members need help that has not been given to them in the past?

Here are a few places to start looking for this information, with examples for an sample audience, plumbers:

- **Water coolers.** These are the informal communities of your niche. This is where they gather without being asked to, where they exchange information freely and without supervision.
- **Facebook groups**, e.g., "Plumbing Hacks And Plumbing Professional Discussions." You might need to work a bit to get into these groups, but explaining that you're interested in helping people and promising not to post advertisements will usually do the trick.
- **Reddit**, e.g., the "Plumbing," "HVAC," and "Construction" subreddits. People ask a lot of questions on Reddit, and they talk very openly about things they dislike.
- **Twitter**, by exploring the #plumbing hashtag and following and engaging with the experts who use it.
- **Self-hosted communities**, like PlumbingZone.com (a forum with over 30,000 professional members) or PlumbersForums.net. Spend a few hours reading the threads and follow all links to further communities and blogs to find the experts and thought leaders, then follow them on social media. The more the community looks like a website from the 90s, the better. Older communities attract and contain a lot of industry veterans.
- **Slack communities.** Many trades and industries have Slack groups where experts interact on a daily basis. Use Slack community discovery platforms

like Slofile or many others[1] to find potential
candidates.

- **Formal communities**. Most trades have some
  organizational bodies like associations and guilds that
  form some sort of virtual community. For our
  example, the "United Association of Journeymen and
  Apprentices of the Plumbing and Pipefitting Industry
  of the United States and Canada" has a website that
  contains a community and listings of subchapters.
  Just sending an email to community representatives
  or a phone call can put you in touch with the right
  people.
- **Event resources**. Find the trade shows and
  conferences of your audience and check out their
  websites. Which vendors were present? What topics
  were discussed? Usually, keynote speakers and their
  talks are listed, if not even recorded.
- **Literature**. Every industry has writers who publish
  papers, books, articles, or comments. Find
  the popular books in the niche[2], read them, or find
  summaries to get a quick glance into the topics they
  cover.

I recommend spending a maximum of an hour for each
audience on your list. Dive as deep as you can into the industry
to see what problems and complaints you can surface. Make a
note of what exists, what doesn't exist, particularly what you
thought would exist but doesn't. This is an indicator of the
potential transfer of knowledge that you might facilitate.

The idea is not to become an expert in every audience candidate on your list. It's about diving deep enough into the field to
see if it can reliably sustain a business. The moment you have a
feeling for this — good or bad — you can stop exploring.

For every row in your audience list, take a few notes about

the problems you encountered (best done outside of the spreadsheet, in a Google Doc or a Notion document), and add another 0–5 value column indicating how interesting those problems sounded to you (with 0 being "there is nothing for me here" and 5 being "this is the most exciting problem space I have ever seen"). Move the rows that don't have exciting problems to another sheet, just like you did with the low-affinity rows.

Aa Audience Name	# Affinity	# Opportunity
Software Engineers	4	4
Bootstrapped Founders	5	5
Non-fiction Authors	5	4
Science-Fiction Fans	4	2
Craft Beer Enthusiasts	3	1
Plumbers & Pipefitters	1	2
Nurses	2	3
Coffee Aficionados	2	1
Book Hoarders	3	1
Miniature Painters	3	2
Progressive Metal Fans	3	1
Lawyers & Notaries	1	4
Aquarium Owners	2	2
Opera Singers	2	3
Heavy Twitter Users	5	4

Ranking the list by opportunity is quite insightful: it becomes clear that there are plenty of audiences with interesting problems, but you don't really care about them too much.

STEP 4: APPRECIATION — FIND OUT IF THEY'RE WILLING TO PAY

In this step, you're trying to figure out if your audience has a budget for solutions to their problem. That's more likely in some audiences than in others: a haircare product supplier business with hundreds of employees will have no problem paying for a customer relationship management software. In contrast, a hairstylist, although they also work in the beauty industry and have to build relationships with their customers, might not have any budget available or wouldn't pay for this at all.

For each audience in your list, look for signs of the following:

- **Purchasing agency:** Can the people you'll be selling to make their own decisions when it comes to buying a professional tool? Will you have to make classic sales, or can you sell in a more low-touch, highly automated way? The less work and the fewer people involved, the better.
- **Budget scope:** What kinds of budgets can your prospective customers in this niche usually spend on products and services? Look into other services that

cater to your prospects to see how they are priced. Think about if people are even aware that they have a budget for professional tools.

In 2017, I co-founded an education-technology Software-as-a-Service business called FeedbackPanda. When I sold the FeedbackPanda product to online teachers, they often didn't even understand that they were self-employed businesspeople. Sometimes, you will need to create awareness within your niche that your prospective customers could improve their tax-efficiency.

The more agency and reliable budgets you find in an audience, the better. If you see people complain about solutions being too expensive or that they should be free, you can usually dismiss that, as these voices appear in any industry. However, if this is the consensus within the communities you find, beware. You might run into walls trying to convince people to exchange money for services here.

For every audience you think is likely to pay or can be convinced to start budgeting for a solution to their problems, add another 0–5 value to their row in your list. Zero means that people are extremely reluctant to pay money for anything, and 5 means that there are plenty of products in the space that people regularly purchase. Move the audiences that have no clear indicator of purchasing intent to another sheet.

Aa Audience Name	# Affinity	# Opportunity	# Appreciation
Software Engineers	4	4	3
Bootstrapped Founders	5	5	4
Non-fiction Authors	5	4	5
Science-Fiction Fans	4	2	1
Craft Beer Enthusiasts	3	1	2
Plumbers & Pipefitters	1	2	3
Nurses	2	3	2
Coffee Aficionados	2	1	2
Book Hoarders	3	1	1
Miniature Painters	3	2	2
Progressive Metal Fans	3	1	3
Lawyers & Notaries	1	4	4
Aquarium Owners	2	2	2
Opera Singers	2	3	2
Heavy Twitter Users	5	4	3

It's often quite interesting how some audiences you may not care about much might be very willing to pay for solutions to their critical problems.

STEP 5: SIZE — FIND OUT IF THIS MARKET CAN SUSTAIN A BUSINESS

The last step to finding a good audience for your sustainable bootstrapped business is to make sure it will be viable. Once you're done with this step, you will end up with a list of businesses that you can build solutions for with a high chance of turning that into a business.

For bootstrappers, a market has to be both large enough to sustain your business and small enough not to attract giant competitors. To find this sweet-spot, the "Goldilocks zone[1]," you will need to know how big your business will have to be to support you. For some founders, this will be $10,000/month in after-tax earnings, while others will need this to be much more or a bit less.

Take that number, double it as a precaution to account for all the unknown unknowns in the market, and divide it by the price you think your audience would pay for your offering. This will be hard to discover, so look for similar products in the space or draw parallels to products in adjacent industries. That will be the number of customers you need to have, at least, to get to your desired income levels.

Let's look at an example. Let's say you need $15,000/month

to support yourself and your family from your SaaS. Doubled, that is $30,000. You have found that in your niche audience of "artisanal beekeepers in New Jersey," the average budget for a bee-tracking SaaS is $15/month max.

You need 2,000 artisanal beekeepers in New Jersey. If you look up the New Jersey Beekeepers Association (and yes, that exists), you find that they have eight chapters with many emails and phone numbers on their website. Call a few of them and tell them that you love beekeeping and would like to help your local honey producers. The person on the other end of the line will be able to tell you immediately if you have your 2,000-people-strong audience or not.

Now, consider that you'll never truly capture 100% of any market. Safety margins differ from industry to industry, so consider that you'll be lucky to turn 10% of that audience into paying customers. It might be more or significantly less. This step is meant to shine a light on the question if it's even possible at all to build a sustainable business within those constraints.

If there aren't enough beekeepers in New Jersey, you might need to zoom out and include other states. If there are too many, you can zoom in and focus on a subset, like hobby beekeepers or beekeepers with more than 10 swarms. That's how you'll find your sweet-spot.

I've done this exercise multiple times, with a lot of industries. It is always very insightful, and once you know the size of a market, you have valuable information, even if you don't get into that particular industry.

Other sources of quickly determining market sizes are:

- social media group user counts
- trade show flyers
- industry reports
- subject matter experts like podcast hosts in the niche

Spend as much time as you need to figure out if an audience is big enough for your business. Then, make sure there are not millions of potential customers in your niche. If you own a small, bootstrapped, sustainable business, you won't have the resources to go up against gigantic competitors with deep pockets. Your niche should not be attractive enough for those businesses.

Looking back at the beekeeper example, if your audience is anywhere between 10,000 and 40,000 beekeepers, that is great. Anything bigger might mean competition from much larger businesses that sense the opportunity to completely take over your niche and serve all beekeepers everywhere.

For each audience on your list, add another 0–5 value indicating if the niche is sized just right for your bootstrapped business aspirations. Five should be a perfectly sized market. Zero is a market that is either way too small or way too big. Move the audiences that don't fit onto another sheet.

Aa Audience Name	# Affinity	# Opportunity	# Appreciation	# Size
Software Engineers	4	4	3	5
Bootstrapped Founders	5	5	4	5
Non-fiction Authors	5	4	5	4
Science-Fiction Fans	4	2	1	2
Craft Beer Enthusiasts	3	1	2	2
Plumbers & Pipefitters	1	2	3	4
Nurses	2	3	2	4
Coffee Aficionados	2	1	2	1
Book Hoarders	3	1	1	1
Miniature Painters	3	2	2	4
Progressive Metal Fans	3	1	3	3
Lawyers & Notaries	1	4	4	4
Aquarium Owners	2	2	2	2
Opera Singers	2	3	2	5
Heavy Twitter Users	5	4	3	4

You will find audiences that might be really problematic to build a business for, no matter how much you might enjoy doing it.

TALLYING THE RESULTS

You now will be left with several audiences that have passed the following checkpoints:

- You're *aware* of the niche.
- You're *interested* in the niche.
- You've found *interesting problems* in the niche.
- You've seen signs from the niche of *interest to pay* for solutions.
- You've found that the niche is *big enough* for your business.

In your spreadsheet, create one final column, adding the point values for each row. Then, sort the whole table so that the highest total point values appear at the top.

A quick side-note: this is only a framework you might want to customize for your own needs. You can add more columns with other considerations or change each column's range of values to reflect how important that particular consideration is to you. At its most basic, this spreadsheet will give you a hint of which audience is the most likely to allow you to build a successful and fulfilling business. I wouldn't overcomplicate this process — and I'm saying this as a software engineer.

Aa Audience Name	# Affinity	# Opportunity	# Appreciation	# Size	Σ Score
Bootstrapped Founders	5	5	4	5	19
Non-fiction Authors	5	4	5	4	18
Software Engineers	4	4	3	5	16
Heavy Twitter Users	5	4	3	4	16
Lawyers & Notaries	1	4	4	4	13
Opera Singers	2	3	2	5	12
Nurses	2	3	2	4	11
Miniature Painters	3	2	2	4	11
Plumbers & Pipefitters	1	2	3	4	10
Progressive Metal Fans	3	1	3	3	10
Science-Fiction Fans	4	2	1	2	9
Craft Beer Enthusiasts	3	1	2	2	8
Aquarium Owners	2	2	2	2	8
Coffee Aficionados	2	1	2	1	6
Book Hoarders	3	1	1	1	6

Looks like I've found a few really interesting audiences. Funny how this book is useful to at least two of them.

With this list, you are ready to choose your audience. Once you have selected one of the items on your list, I suggest doing another deep dive into the industry. Read up on the history of the trade, see who already sells into the industry, and how they speak to their customers.

After this point, you will stick with your audience and focus on helping them solve their problems. Finding and validating their critical problem is your next objective. Once you have done that, you can work on your solution and implement your product — knowing that you are building for a validated audience.

The great thing about this exercise is that you don't only end up with a few fascinating audiences to get started with right away, but you also have all those other audiences that got excluded during some steps along the way. In the future, either when you sell your business or when the world changes in a significant way, you'll already have new audiences waiting to be explored again, with fresh eyes. It's a backlog of pre-validated audiences that you know you could serve. This will be a great backup resource that you can use if you're running into problems in the future.

But for now, stick with the audience that the data says is the best choice. Dive deep into the communities and tribes, and figure out what those people need help with. From there, you can build a sustainable business that solves their problem in a validated fashion, without any guesswork.

AWARENESS

AFFINITY

OPPORTUNITY

APPRECIATION

SIZE

AUDIENCE EXPLORATION

TO BOLDLY GO WHERE NO
ENTREPRENEUR HAS GONE BEFORE

> We shall not cease from exploration, and the end of all our exploring will be to arrive where we started and know the place for the first time.

T. S. ELIOT

Once you have chosen an audience to serve and empower, you'll need to learn more about them. The goal of the Audience Exploration phase is to understand your audience's motivations and move yourself into a position where you can detect an unsolved problem that you can build a business around.

There is no clear line between Audience Discovery and Audience Exploration. In fact, if you followed the five-step Audience Discovery guide, you already did a little bit of exploration while you were looking into opportunities for each audience. Audience Discovery and Audience Exploration can happen together at the same time. Or you might choose to do neither exercise and simply keep a lookout for opportunities that match the patterns introduced in those chapters. Some founders go back and forth between these phases, while others try to go through them in order.

The important thing to remember with these exercises is that they are designed to bring you closer to your future audience — both in a sense of proximity and empathetically.

First, you need to understand where to find your prospects.

That's where Embedded Exploration comes into play: you will become an Embedded Entrepreneur. This is the core concept of Audience Exploration and will be introduced in this chapter.

The Embedded Exploration phase ends when you have established yourself in several communities that your audience frequents and have started a note-taking routine about commonly experienced issues and challenges. If you're planning to build a business on the side, this is a long-term activity that you can do while you're working a day job.

EMBEDDED EXPLORATION

During your initial exploration of the audience that you're willing to serve, you will have dipped your toes into a few communities to see if there are large enough markets and sufficient opportunities. That first glance will have uncovered the tip of the iceberg, but there is much more. The Embedded Exploration approach, when applied intentionally and consistently, will structure a large part of your entrepreneurial journey.

OBSERVE
PROBLEMS

EMBEDDED
EXPLORATION

1

SaaS

B2B

LEARN HOW PEOPLE
COMMUNICATE

2

OBSERVE
SUCCESS

3

ENGAGE WITH
COMMUNITY

4

Here's the quick summary:

- You will find and embed yourself in your audience's communities. That's where it starts, and that is what this chapter is all about.
- You will discover real and painful problems from within the communities. The **Problem Discovery** chapters will go into great detail on how this can be done in practice.
- You will leverage those communities to become a domain expert and a reputable contributor over time. This will set you apart from the existing competition. We'll dive deep into how you can build this brand in the **Audience-Building** chapters.
- With these three steps in motion, you will collaborate with your audience to create a business built on trust and meaningful relationships.

Sounds like a lot, right? It really isn't. It's just a matter of approaching business from a human-centric angle.

Many classical economic theories deal in numbers and statistics exclusively, but there is a reversion towards reputational and relational work in the indie and creator economies. Humans matter; people are not just voiceless consumers. More and more, people ignore hard facts and figures, and seek softer "metrics": they look for empathy, kinship, kindness, and connection.

Now that you have decided which audience you want to serve and empower, you can start "getting out of the building," discover where your prospective customers hang out and join them in their communities where you can understand and solve their problems. There is a research methodology in the social sciences called "the ethnographic method," which is very similar to what we're planning to do here: the researcher joins a cultural setting, observes actively (by directly being part of the social activities), and passively (by surveying the actions of others from a distance), and then forms a narrative account of what they learned, contrasting it to an initial theoretical assumption. Embedded Exploration borrows from that method.

Through Embedded Exploration, you will dive deep into existing communities. You will become an "Embedded Community Observer": someone who joins a community to learn as much as possible about the people in it and the day-to-day problems they encounter. You're embedding yourself to become an expert in the subject matter of your target audience.

Keep in mind that we are not yet at the stage where we actively try to sell something to our audience. In this section, we're looking at these platforms as an observational researcher. We're not building an audience; we're investigating it. We'll dive deeper into the day-to-day actions and strategies for audience-building later. Right now, we focus on conversations, problems, and insights.

It all starts with "lurking," the practice of passively observing an active community. When you first enter such a group, you're an unknown factor, and you won't be attuned to the ongoing conversations just yet. You might not even understand what people are discussing. To prevent you from crashing and burning by saying something unreflected too soon, I recommend you join communities and stay silent for a while. Asking thoughtful questions is fine. Barraging a community with your opinions is not.

In the meantime, you can start collecting content that you can either re-contribute (through sharing and commenting) or absorb to gain a deeper understanding of the community. Take note of links and resources that are being shared in the community and curate them in a database of your own. You'll also have the chance to learn who the influential people are in the group and start connecting with them.

Once you understand the jargon that people use and have interesting things to contribute, you should engage the community. After all, direct conversations — in public or in private — will allow you to learn exactly what you need to know to start building solutions to people's problems. By connecting people, sharing your observations and learnings freely, and being a person that others want to interact with, you'll start building a following for yourself.

During your Embedded Exploration in a community, you will be focusing on these activities:

- Observe pain, problems, and challenges. Note down common themes and insights.
- Learn how people communicate. Find the phrases and jargon they use that others don't.
- Look for people who sell successfully. How are they wording their pitches? What have they understood about your audience that you haven't yet? If communities don't allow selling: how do people involve others in their projects?
- Engage with community members to find verifiable first-hand accounts and build relationships.

So, with your notebook, your eyes, and your ears open, let's dive into Embedded Exploration.

COMMUNITIES

Finding Communities

You can't observe and talk to people without knowing where they can be found. The initial step of Embedded Exploration is to find the place of professional exchange: the proverbial water cooler. By the way, "professional exchange" isn't limited to actual business audiences. Consider craft beer enthusiasts. They have animated discussions in communities, groups, and forums, yet drinking craft beer is not a salaried profession. Wherever there is expertise, there is a water cooler.

I already mentioned a few potential locations in the Opportunity step of the Audience Discovery guide, and we'll dive deep into each one — and a few more. Before we get to the specifics, let's first explore this step's goal and what kinds of communities you can expect to find.

The goal is to end up with a list of at least five communities to engage your audience actively. In the end, you will very likely restrict your efforts to one or two communities, but to find the best ones, you will need to know all of your options first. I recommend making a list of every single community you find while you research them. No matter if you end up joining those communities or not, this list itself might be interesting content that marks you as a domain expert in the future. It's a useful resource to create early on.

For inspiration, visit community exploration tool resources like The Hive Index and find your initial communities to embed yourself in. If you can't find anything there, don't worry. Community discovery will be a cakewalk once you understand how communities work.

Kinds of Communities

You can categorize communities depending on two properties: their purpose (the "why") and their platform (the "where"). Both properties make a big difference in how you should approach embedding yourself into that community. I'll point out the significant differences between these archetypical communities and what to keep in mind when you engage with the people in them.

We will look into the following kinds of communities:

- Goal-driven communities
- Practice-driven communities
- Interest-driven communities
- Location-driven communities
- Circumstance-driven communities
- Hybrids

Goal-Driven Communitites

These communities form around a common cause. Social progress, achieving certain milestones, making a difference:

these are the themes around which these communities form. Members of these communities are expected to further the goals with their actions. Your reputation is determined by the alignment of your publicly stated goals and actions with the community goal. Any deviation or selfishness will cause a lot of reputational damage.

Examples of these communities would be sustainability-driven Facebook groups, the minimalism subreddit, or climate-change forums.

Consider educating and encouraging members in these communities. Anything that accelerates the cause is welcome, so contribute time and resources to the group's goals. Goal-driven communities are very cautious when it comes to overt advertisements, as most causes are notoriously under-funded. Most marketing is seen as reducing the number of resources that the community can use. The only kind of marketing these groups will accept is word-of-mouth marketing that is free of incentives. The moment people smell a referral system or any other self-centered motivation, administrators will remove the content. If you encourage other community members to talk about your product, clarify that it has to come from an honest place.

Finding problems in these communities is best attempted by keeping a lookout for roadblocks. Whenever people want to act in the group's interest but can't, there is a potential problem for you to solve. Are people trying to organize a conference but just can't get it done? Are they trying to share certain documents with each other, but they are just emailing them back and forth? Look for things that stand in the way of reaching the commonly shared goal.

Not all problems are resource issues: sometimes, information organization or easier access to specific tools or people can make a big difference. Consider how you can help every single member of this group to make better contributions to the common goal.

Practice-Driven Communities

In practice-driven communities, people usually do the same things. They work the same job, or they are experts in the same field. Expertise is at the core of those groups. Members are expected to further the group's collective knowledge. Conversations in these groups are usually centered around "doing things right," finding and illuminating proven best practices, elevating new experts, and exposing newly discovered charlatans. These groups' focus is to provide resources and encouragement to members of all skill levels, intending to turn every member into an expert eventually.

The community that my co-founder Danielle and I embedded in for our SaaS FeedbackPanda was such a practice-driven community. It was a Facebook group of Online English Teachers who were teaching for a particular kind of school. In the group, they would exchange a lot of guidance on becoming a successful and prolific teacher. A similar community is the BaristaExchange, where professional bartenders talk about how best to serve their customers.

These communities enjoy their members sharing and discussing the finer points of their practice as well as introducing new members to the best practices of their industry. If you are already an expert, share your expertise freely, and if you are a relative beginner, consider engaging the community with questions. In a group of experts that aims to educate, people will respond to questions as they are a public method of education for those who might have the same questions or will run into them in the future.

Practice-driven communities are always watching for new and interesting things, as these innovations could result in a new best practice or general improvement to the industry. By freely sharing news and experimental approaches, you can contribute to the discussion and prompt experts to engage with you. It pays to be considered as someone who shares an interest in collective improvement.

Sharing your progress is a proven way to keep engaged with such a community continuously. As people are interested in learning, they see someone publicly documenting their journey to expertise as a chance to gauge how effective their teaching is. At the same time, other learners see themselves reflected in your experience and will follow you for that reason.

Interest-Driven Communities

Similarly, communities form around people who like the same things, who have the same hobbies, or who engage in the same activities. Unlike in practice-driven communities, however, the primary motivation for people to interact here is passion. Expertise matters, too, but a member who is passionate about the shared interest will be welcomed with open arms any day, no matter how little they know about the topic. Conversations in these communities are just as much about passion as they are passionate. This can lead to a lot of polarization and "going down rabbit holes," in regular exchanges of opinion. Try staying out of the more combative conversations. You're not there to fight but to observe and analyze.

When people care deeply about something, they often conflate the thing with their identity. A lot of bonding and posturing happens when like-minded people talk about their favorite things. Your reputation will be measured by how much you embrace your identity as an in-group person. Understanding and using the particular language — the "jargon" — of this community will be an integral part of this. Paying particular attention to the words and phrases people use will also enable you to tailor your messaging to the in-group people in the future.

You can find examples of this type of community on Reddit. Almost every niche subreddit is an interest-driven community. When people talk about keeping ducks in their backyard, share pictures of tonight's dinner, or post videos of cats that yell, you can be quite sure to have found a group of people who sincerely enjoy discussing one particular kind of thing.

This kind of similarity between group members can be highly beneficial for your problem exploration process. Provided that you're looking at a community where people actually have problems — I'm not sure if any interest in yelling cats results in any significant problems — you'll be quickly able to see if those problems are commonly experienced. Critical problems are usually experienced by a majority of your audience. If you see complaints about a particular issue crop up very often within an interest-driven community, that's indicative of a painful problem that is felt by many.

The best way to engage with an interest-driven community is to be interested and interesting. Encouraging community members to share their stories and successes is a reliable way to build a reputation. Sharing opinion pieces and inviting discussion is expected from active community members. Anything that engages new and old community members alike is well-received.

Location-Driven Communitites

In the past, almost every community was limited by location. You could only connect with the people around you, which was very limiting but also more direct than the infinite web of virtual connections an individual can establish in the digital age. In modern life, local communities have transcended the physical world and moved into online spaces. The purpose stays the same: connect people from a particular place. These groups are focused on local events, the exchange of goods or services within certain geographical boundaries, or providing support to each other.

Neighborhood platforms like NextDoor are a great example, aimed at providing people with trustworthy connections. There are also many professional associations like the United Association of Journeymen and Apprentices of the Plumbing, Pipefitting and Sprinkler Fitting Industry of the United States and Canada (that's a handful, right?) that have location-based branches and sub-communities like the New Jersey division. Every industry has thousands of these location-bounded communities at varying levels of the geographical area covered.

Trust is the currency of location-driven communities. Like in the days before the internet, a person's reputation depended on their acceptance by their local community. Location-driven communities work the same way. If the locals do not know you, you're an outsider, untrustworthy by default.

Trust takes time to be given. It's earned. For a genuine outsider, this will be hard. Knowing someone on the inside to introduce you into the community is often the only way to get some "trust traction." The only other way is actually being part of the local community both in the virtual and the physical space. Visiting trade shows, meetups, fairs, and conferences will give you access to the real people who will then recognize you in the digital realm.

Location-driven communities often operate on reciprocation. One member helps the other, only to be supported by another member at some future point. You'll get the most out of these communities by selflessly assisting other members. Reciprocity is a very storable good. People will remember being helped by you years after you did it, and they'll be willing to assist you in your own efforts.

Generally, location-driven communities are exciting observation targets for niche audiences. Particularly if you join a few different location-based communities, you will learn a lot about the differences in otherwise very similar groups' problems and needs. You can use this insight to pinpoint the market you ultimately want to operate in. If you see an abundance of one particular problem in all groups, you can serve the encompassing market. If one particular location experiences a critical problem even more substantially than others, they might be a great initial audience for your tailored solution.

Circumstance-Driven Communities

Sometimes, unexpected things happen to people. That usually causes them to seek other people who are experiencing the same problems. They support each other, guiding new group members through the challenging stages of whatever they are experiencing. Usually, it is some form of hardship or challenge, like a medical or psychological condition. Other times, it's a marginalized group of people empowering each other.

In all cases, circumstance-driven communities focus on the bonding between members and supporting members along their journey of overcoming the challenge. More than in other communities, personal relationships play a central role here. Finding acceptance and the comfort of others is the reason why people join these groups. The initial motivation is to cope with something threatening. Be particularly careful with anything that could remotely look like advertising. Communities that aim to connect people can smell a marketer from five clicks away — and they will ban you faster than you can post a link to your site. Use these communities to observe. If you engage with people, make it about them, not about you.

Some communities of circumstance are temporary. When events occur that impact the lives of many, the affected people will try to cooperate in such a community until the event and its aftermath are dealt with. Think of people displaced by forest fires or stuck at home during a national lockdown. These communities have a shelf-life and often evaporate or slowly fade away after a while. This means that you should constantly be on the lookout for new circumstance-driven communities in your market.

These kinds of communities are abundantly packed with problems and complaints. They're a treasure trove for audience analysis and critical problem detection. You can help surface these issues by engaging with the people in the group and asking about their stories. If you genuinely care about your audience, this will be a great opportunity to connect with real people and their real experiences.

Hybrid Communities are the Norm

You will quickly find that no community is a perfect example of the archetypes mentioned above. There is no "pure practice-driven community" that wouldn't also include interest-driven conversations. Most communities are a mix of different purposes, like a spider diagram. In particular, larger communities tick most of the boxes, just from the sheer number of different voices inside them. Many purposes can coexist in one large group of people.

In fact, not only do communities fluctuate between different purposes, but they also change over time, often significantly. Depending on who moderates and steers the conversation, a community of interest might professionalize into a practice-driven community, for example. It depends on the people who make up the community and what they ultimately want to accomplish.

Over-eager purism usually deteriorates communities. If moderators suppress anything that is not entirely on-topic, users will feel patronized and quickly look for greener pastures.

Administrators and community leaders will usually allow some levels of deviation. Try not to be the one to test those boundaries, though. Whenever you feel like a message you want to put to the community might be unexpected or might be considered hostile, check how others have communicated similar content before. If you can't find any such examples, that is a good indicator that you might not want to send the message.

Professional or Recreational

There is also an interesting distinction between two kinds of community "levels of professionalism." People congregate either for recreation or in a professional setting. While the same people can inhabit those groups, communication patterns change.

Take, for example, how group hierarchy is determined. Signaling that you have the proper credentials (either as documents or peer reputation) will elevate you to the level of expert in a professional group. When you're in a recreational group, these hierarchies are usually irrelevant. Demonstrated expertise and dedication are appreciated much more than showing people that you're more qualified than they are.

A word about dedication: online communities usually attract people who just *have* to talk about the things they're interested in. It's a form of self-selection to join such a community: there is a minimum threshold of passion you need in order to be regularly active in such a community. Compare that with a job: we show up because we get paid to do it. If we don't regularly contribute, we lose the job. Voluntary community membership is different.

What does that mean? The average online community member will be more enthusiastic about their niche's ins and outs than the average general member of that audience or market. Consider this when you explore problems and opinions. You're dealing with people that have self-selected to be the voice of their community. That can be a good thing, as they will likely amplify your message throughout the community, but it can also mean that your research will be slightly skewed towards their specific interests.

THE FOUR PRINCIPLES OF EMBEDDED EXPLORATION

Before we look into the actual communities that you can embed yourself into, let's be absolutely clear about the goal and the four basic activities that this process consists of.

The goal is to find as many high-quality communities and content locations as possible, so you can investigate problems, challenges, and needs in these communities. What you want to end up with is a list of communities and an account in each of them.

From there, you should aim to conduct these four main activities at all times:

1. Find the community experts, follow them, and follow those who engage them.
2. Find breakout communities and follow the conversation.
3. Engage the Engaged. Reach out to people who are particularly active and insightful.
4. Make notes of common themes and complaints.

For each community, I will answer two central questions:

- How can you spot problems and challenges in this community?
- What questions should you ask the members of this community?

Now, let's look into how you can do this in real communities with real people.

COMMUNITY PLATFORMS

Now that you know what kinds of communities you can expect to find, let's look at where to find them and what needs to be considered for maximum results. Some examples will fit into their category perfectly, while others are blurring the line. For each community you look at, I will point out why you want to embed yourself there, how to do that efficiently, and what you can expect to find.

I'll show you a lot of different community platforms and variants, and share plenty of insights for each. This might be overwhelming, but take this as an opportunity to gauge how much you resonate with each of these communities. In the end, you will focus only on a handful of them. I believe that it's good to know the basics of each before you commit to any.

Social Media Communities

The one thing that unites all social media platforms is that there is usually a feed. It could be a news feed, an activity feed, the latest events, something that is the medium's central focus. Around that feed, social connections thrive. People's identity is usually public, and creating personal relationships is expected and encouraged. Conversations on social media often center on experiences of people and less on abstract topics.

Social media platforms allow for communities to form inside their own large community. Some social media platforms allow for creating intentional sub-communities, while others trust that the network effect between connected community members is enough to form communities. Facebook has billions of users and an equally impressive amount of distinct groups. On the other hand, Twitter has millions of users, but it does not allow for the creation of differentiated groups: your community is who you follow. Some communities are temporary, like ad-hoc Telegram groups, and others are persistent and well-searchable, like YouTube channels. Different structures require different behaviors and will create different expectations.

Facebook

With almost three billion users, Facebook is *the* social network. Everyone and their mother is on Facebook — literally. That's the reason this network is so ubiquitous: from the start, people transferred their personal network onto the social media platform, and people of all ages use it to stay connected with their friends and loved ones.

Because of this, there are all kinds and sizes of communities on Facebook. Many are organized in Facebook groups, and those are the communities you want to embed yourself in. They are very often extremely specific, which is very helpful when you already know which niche you want to serve.

Generally, you will discover interesting groups using the Facebook search bar or using the more specific search bar in the Groups section. The more you know about your audience, the better: try searching using specific keywords. For example, if I were to look for groups related to self-published authors, I'd search for "self-publishing," "KDP" (the Amazon Platform for self-published authors), and "independent writer." I'd then pick the most populated and active groups to join.

There are also a large number of location-driven communities on Facebook. You can filter by a city when you search for groups, which will show you only the communities either named after that city or with a majority of members from that city. This will be very useful for sub-niche research.

Here's the issue: the most interesting groups are invite-only. Getting into those groups will require a bit of work, and it won't be guaranteed that you'll be able to join. The people who moderate those communities consider it their mission to keep their communities safe. They will employ plenty of scrutiny when someone new wants to join their group.

I have found that you can tip the scales in your favor by being strategic. To join and stay in these groups:

1. Learn as much as you can about the administrators and prepare a compelling and honest message for your join request. You will want to point out your motivation: learning more about the problems and challenges that people in the community face.
2. Be clear that you'll be an observer and student, not a marketer. If you can, provide proof from other groups that you mean no harm.
3. Show that you've been part of similar communities in the past.
4. Social proof is everything on social media. You can leverage that.

Once you are in a group, it's generally hard to search for past content, but you can do it. Particularly in the first few days after joining, I recommend stepping through the last few weeks of conversation history and learning both the jargon and the themes that show up. You might want to note down common themes and complaints, as those are the pieces of content that you can engage with to learn more about perceived problems in the community. Once you're up-to-date, visit your Facebook groups daily and either note down or take screenshots of the most interesting messages and conversations.

Joining groups requires some work already, but connecting with people is even more challenging. Many people on Facebook consider it to be a personal network of real-life acquaintances. While they will join groups without much of a question, they will be very hesitant to connect with you as a Facebook "friend." For that, you will need to build a personal relationship inside the groups first, and even then, many people might refuse to connect with you. Consider Facebook to be a research-only place for now. While you can eventually use the platform for marketing and audience-building, for the embedding part of your entrepreneurial journey, you might want to stick to observation only.

A few Facebook Group Discovery tools are trying to improve the experience provided by the internal Facebook search, such as TargetSnake. What you can do beyond using these tools is ask people directly on Facebook about what other Facebook groups they would recommend for you to join. This may have fascinating results: some groups are oddly named and very hard to discover. You'll never find them without asking. Consider asking for invitations, too: it's so much easier to join a closed group when a member asks for you to be added.

When it comes to engagement, try to be conversational. A post with many comments attracts more engagement, which is something every Facebook user values. By commenting and asking questions, you will invite more discussion and build relationships with the other users: they'll get to know you as a curious and inquisitive community member, and you'll understand what they care about.

Learn about the rules of each community right after you join. Some forbid all kinds of marketing, even market research. Other communities don't allow certain topics to be discussed. Make sure you abide by the rules at all times. When you wonder if your post goes against those guidelines, reach out to a group moderator. That will help you avoid making mistakes and build a relationship of respect and trust between you and the people who have control over the community.

Eventually, you will be able to ask questions in the group and get another member to comment. Since Facebook posts don't have a maximum length, you can be very clear about your intention. Don't just ask one-liner questions. Be precise about why you are asking, what you are most interested in. If people understand that you're there to learn, they will put as much effort into their replies as you put into your questions.

When I was running the EdTech productivity SaaS Feed-backPanda with my partner Danielle, Facebook groups were the dominant online community where our audience hung out. We regularly checked the conversations that were going on to find new problems that teachers were facing and then engaged with the people in the comments to learn about the specifics. We stuck to commenting on posts since we wanted to avoid directly asking people for their problems. The thought here was that if a problem is painful enough, people will talk about it without being asked to. Asking for a list of problems might remove that indicator of urgency.

Once we had a product that we wanted to sell to these groups' members, we carefully commented on questions where dropping the link to our website was a clear response. We avoided talking about the product in any other conversations. We encouraged people who shared the link to our landing page — usually with a like or a friendly "thank you" message. But we never blatantly asked people to check out our business. That would have gone against the community rules as much as it would have been a selfish move — both unacceptable behavior in Facebook groups.

Here's a quick summary of how to embed yourself in Facebook groups:

- Invite-only groups: make a case for why you're a good fit, use social proof.
- Ask people for other group recommendations and to invite you.
- Observe the frequency of problem mentions on a daily basis.
- Comment on people's posts with engaging questions.
- Ask straightforward questions and provide context.
- Use Direct Messages to deeply engage with people who you have found to be helpful to your cause.

Let's look at our two central questions:

- How can you spot problems and challenges in this community?
- Look out for complaints that receive a lot of likes and comments agreeing with the poster. These are commonly shared issues.
- Observe which questions get asked over and over again by people who have recently joined that Facebook groups. These indicate a learning or understanding barrier.
- Note which companies pay money to advertise to members of particular Facebook groups. They likely have found them to be a susceptible audience.
- What questions should you ask the members of this community?
- "What problems do you run into over and over again? Has anyone tried to solve them before?"

- "Do you spend money on solutions to the problems discussed here?"
- "Who should I reach out to if I want to learn more about this industry/field?"
- "Where else on Facebook can I find people who have issue X? Are there any other groups you can recommend?"

Twitter

The short-message-based social network platform Twitter is a real treasure trove for embedded exploration efforts. It's a highly interconnected web of relationships and conversations, and many interesting tools are available for your audience research.

Twitter has a firehose feed: once you follow a few hundred active people, every page refresh will show you new tweets. Even more than Facebook, this means that content comes and goes, and unless you're prepared to take notes, it might vanish very quickly. When you do Twitter-based research, get used to copying the link to individual interesting tweets into a link collection document as soon as you read them. If you don't, you might have trouble locating those tweets later.

The feed consists of all the tweets written by the Twitter accounts you follow. The more people you follow, the more content you get to see. To observe a community, you will have to follow as many members of that community as possible.

On Twitter, there are no distinct groups as they exist on Facebook. Communities are established through constant inter-action, by people following each other and engaging with each other's tweets. While replies are often used to continue conver-sations, retweets and quote tweets (which are retweets with an added message) amplify content and invite conversations in the first place. Depending on if you follow someone who interacts with any particular discussion happening in a community, you may or may not see it in your Twitter feed.

Thankfully, this is a solvable problem. Twitter acquired a tool called TweetDeck back in 2011, which you can use for free. Not only does TweetDeck give you access to the full feed for your account, but you can also build secondary feeds that you can set up to only show tweets mentioning particular phrases or users. If you're serious about observing a Twitter community, you need to set up keyword monitoring to pull your attention to these conversations when they happen.

Still, you will need to follow people from your audience to find the full extent of their community. It takes a while to find all the active accounts in any given niche. What works best for me whenever I do audience research on Twitter is to find the influencers and follow interesting people they interact with. Then, I look into the followers those people interact with and follow them. It's a rabbit hole, but it results in a very extensive graph of relationships — which is exactly what Twitter is about.

The term "influencer" has been used to ridicule superficial opportunists who project a fake version of success and glamor to eventually sell their own brand of hand creme. On Twitter, there are quite a few of those people, but when I talk about influencers in the context of communities, I mean something else: people who have a lot of reputation and the power to steer conversations in any given niche community. Niche influencers are genuine community members who have risen to their influential position by providing value to their communities. Among software developers, the people who have been teachers or contributors to open-source projects for many years often become influencers. In the Online Teaching community, people who connect teachers and empower them to become better at their jobs rise to fame. Find the teachers, find the community members who unite their community, and find the nexus of communication and a massive amount of follower accounts that you can follow yourself.

Twitter has a feature called "Lists," where accounts can be followed as a batch. Lists can be named and searched for, which makes this a great way of quickly discovering large numbers of high-quality accounts. Most influential Twitter users are on lists like "Awesome Marketers" or "Women in Tech." Just like when you looked into an influencer's followers to find new accounts to follow, check out their lists and follow the ones you find interesting.

The true scale of a community won't be apparent from the start. Only consistent exposure to the conversations on Twitter will make things clear to you. You'll learn who is talking about topics you care about. Twitter only works because of engagement. Observe the Twitter accounts that create a lot of engagement. What stories do they share? What links do they post? This will lead you to communities outside of Twitter as well.

Unlike Facebook, Twitter is very timezone-dependent as everyone's feed quickly replaces older items with new tweets. Depending on where you are located, you might miss a large part of the conversation because it happens while you sleep and gets pushed down by other content before you wake up. This makes tracking keywords and phrases you care about even more important, as this will allow you to find these conversations more easily.

Hashtags used to be all the rage in Twitter's early days but are barely used now and can't be relied upon for discovery. Mostly used by brands that have not yet understood how modern Twitter works, they often indicate naïve and cheap Twitter marketing efforts and are eschewed by professional Twitter users. More casual Twitter users will still use hashtags, mainly when they are talking about current events.

Don't discount hashtags for discovering communities of location or circumstance. The same goes for movements like

"Building in Public," which often uses the #BuildInPublic hashtag for people to understand the implied purpose of particular tweets. That would be a prime example of a community of practice coalescing around a hashtag.

It's important to understand that conversations on Twitter are usually public exchanges between a handful of people. Rarely can a discussion be maintained if more than five or six people are actively debating a topic. For Twitter users with huge followings, this means that quite often, any discussion they instigate turns into thousands of people trying to get the influencer's attention. It can be exhausting to analyze these conversations, which is why you're better off learning how to use the Twitter Advanced Search[1] and searching for replies by the influencer within the responses to their own tweets.

Also, all content being public means that any engagement you do will be highly visible to others. Always consider the impact of your words and responses on your followers. As with any ethnographic research method, consider the implications your actions may have on the group of people you're observing.

Since most things on Twitter happen in public, many tools have sprung up that give the budding entrepreneur insight into accounts, relationships, and topics on the platform. Here are a few that I use to do my audience research:

- **SparkToro:** Rand Fishkin, the founder of Moz and writer of Lost and Founder, built this service to allow founders and marketers to find out what their audience consumes, talks about, and who they follow. Beyond that, the business offers free tools to find trending topics and audit individual accounts. Use SparkToro to find out who to follow in your niche and what they talk about.
- **BuzzSumo:** Spotting the influencers means finding the core conversation amplifiers. Those are the

people you need to follow and engage with to access the larger community. BuzzSumo helps you find them quickly.

- There are hundreds of interesting tools that interact with Twitter[2]. Searching for "Twitter Discovery Tool" will show you the ones that are most likely to assist your embedded exploration.

A quick word about Twitter's secret weapon, Direct Messages (DMs). Twitter is unique, as it allows you to send a Direct Message to anyone who either follows you or has public DMs activated. This means that you will be able to write a personal, point-blank message to any Twitter account that you want. This is incredibly powerful, particularly as the conversation in DMs will be much more private than the public tweet/response conversations. There is a proven strategy of following interesting people, engaging with them often and honestly, having them follow you back eventually, and then building a more personal relationship through Twitter DMs. Over time, these relationships can turn into opportunities, both for immediate insights and for your business in the future. While during Embedded Exploration, this will likely turn into conversations about the other person's problems and insights, at a later point, you'll have pre-warmed relationships that can either turn into customers or amplifiers for your messaging. It's never wrong to build personal connections on Twitter.

Here's a summary of how you can use Twitter to embed yourself into a community:

- Find and follow influencers, then follow the lists they're on and the lists they curate. Follow their most engaged followers, too, then repeat.
- Consistently follow conversations to explore the whole breadth of the Twitter community.

- Note down interesting conversations by copying the link to individual tweets.
- Leverage Direct Messages to build personal relationships with domain experts from your audience.

Let's look at our two central questions and how you can answer them for Twitter:

- How can you spot problems and challenges in this community?
- Find the big names in the industry, follow them, and follow those who are highly engaged with problem-surfacing tweets. The chances are that all involved parties will talk a lot about the day-to-day issues in their fields.
- Use Twitter tools to be notified when certain keywords show up in your feed. With TweetDeck, try "problem," "issue," and "can't understand."
- What questions should you ask the members of this community?
- "How do you solve problem X?"[3]
- "Who else here on Twitter is an expert in this field?"[4]
- "What issues are people complaining about most often? Who is the most vocal advocate for change?"
- "Do you know any resources where these issues are discussed in more detail?"
- "What players are similar to X, but for the Y audience?"[5]

Instagram

One of the most visual social networks, Instagram can also be used for audience exploration, even though public communities are not represented well by the platform. Hashtags are used to categorize content, and the ability to follow specific hashtags will create community-like structures around those keywords. But beyond exchanging visual content and the respective comments on each post, public discussions don't happen as much as they do on the more text-based social media.

Instagram is very influencer-centric. Users with large followings have power over what is currently being discussed. The medium's visual nature tends to favor concrete conversational themes (as opposed to more abstract and theoretical discussions that often occur on other social media platforms). This is very useful when researching a niche: people will often share more than the main focus of the image or video. Their screenshots will show what other software is installed on their computers, their photos of the food they consume will show what appliances they have in their kitchens. Instagram is spectacular for exploring the context in which your audience operates. Collect visual impressions of what the real life of your audience looks like.

When it comes to groups to join, you don't have many options. The only equivalent of private conversations happens in Direct Messages and through "Finstas": Fake Instagram accounts used to share more intimate stories and images. Since Instagram accounts are usually very curated and edited, many Instagram users use Finsta accounts for more vulnerable and realistic content. This will be hard to find, but insights will be so much more valuable once you have access to the real story.

So, how do you find the people who might give you these insights? Start at the top. Find the brands and well-known influencers, and follow who they follow and interact with. Tools like the Phlanx Influencer Auditor will help find more detailed information about engagement rates and follower compositions.

Instagram is — like most social media platforms because

they monetize through ads that need constant engagement — a place where older content quickly gets replaced by new posts. Observing such a platform means that you'll need to check for new content quite regularly, at least on a daily basis. Once you follow a sufficiently large group of people, take note of which topics are being discussed regularly. Instagram search is limited to hashtags and users, so prepare to take screenshots and save individual links.

Since Instagram introduced Stories, more candid conversations have cropped up around them. Influencers who have very polished visuals allow themselves to be more relatable in the video content. The transient nature of Instagram Stories — the fact that they are automatically deleted after a while — is leveraged to create more urgency for engagement. Simultaneously, being more vulnerable and "real" on stories keeps people coming back for more. You'll want to pay attention to the themes and topics covered in the stories that circulate within your target audience. There are tools available that allow you to download and persist those stories[6].

Let's look at our two central questions:

- How can you spot problems and challenges in this community?
- Take the polished visual content for what it is: more fiction than fact. Look for truth in the genuine interactions between Instagram users in the comments, and look for Stories where creators are more honest about their lives.
- Find the external communication platforms where influencers assemble their communities.
- What questions should you ask the members of this community?
- "Who else has genuine insights into this community?"

- To the influencer: "What problems do you see bother the majority of your followers?"
- "Where do people who enjoy this content hang out?"

Pinterest

Where Instagram is all about the reality of people's lives — however much it's distorted by filters and staged photos — Pinterest is the inspirational perspective. On Pinterest, users share images and links of things they want, like, and aspire to. Pinterest is less about the personal experience than communicating desires and insights visually.

Many Pinterest users don't actively engage with the content. They use it as a visual search engine only. For influencers, that matters very little, as long as people engage with their content (that's often monetized through affiliate links). For that reason, you will find comments and any kind of discussion lacking on this platform. Still, for many audiences, it might allow you to find useful visuals through which to understand your niche better.

Pinterest users use boards to group their thematically similar content together. Following these boards will expose you to fresh content when it is released. You'll also get a general feeling for the communication approach that resonates with your target audience members. Find common themes and which communication patterns work best, and make a note to use them in your own marketing in the future. Over the years, prolific Pinterest users have also learned how to give their pins well-performing SEO titles and descriptions. You can imitate those at a later point for an easy start into the world of SEO.

Sidenote: Cross-Community Communications

Influencers and popular account owners on all social media platforms have understood one thing: the platform owns the relationships. The risk of losing everything grows with the number of followers an account has. A platform can quite arbitrarily remove or limit access to any account for any reason they might have. Consequentially, influencers have understood that they are better off taking their community someplace else, having a second way of communicating with them should they be de-platformed.

For that reason, many high-follower accounts have started funneling the most active of their followers into private Messenger groups, onto Discord and Slack servers, all places where direct communication can happen without the involvement of the social media platform. Even though these services are also for-profit businesses, engaging an audience on multiple channels with different kinds of communication is a tangible way of distribution channel diversification.

Being on another platform changes how people approach communication. Comments on Instagram or replies on Twitter are public. People communicate differently when they know that strangers are watching, even if it's just potentially. Once they are in a closed community, behavior patterns change. People build meaningful relationships, become more candid, and talk about topics in this semi-private medium that they are too frightened to mention on the public social media platforms.

For Embedded Exploration, this is a gold mine. You couldn't get a more homogeneously aligned group of people talking candidly in a central location to learn about their problems and needs. If you find such a group, join it. These communities' internal structure will also give you very interesting insights into how the community understands itself. The kinds of channels and breakout sessions that exist in any given community say a lot about how it perceives itself. Some communities are very exclusive and elitist, while others warmly invite newcomers into their midst. That mindset will give you actionable insights into how to communicate with that particular audience.

Whenever you see such a cross-platform communication suggestion, I recommend two things: take a note from which platform and account to which platform this particular audience has been shifted, and then join that new platform. The access you'll have to other audience members will be so much better and provide you with more interesting opportunities to observe real-talk conversations.

YouTube

The video platform YouTube looks very one-directional: creators publish videos, and viewers consume them. But it's quite different once you start looking under the hood of many communities. The YouTube comments on popular videos are often full of trolls and negativity. In smaller niches, however, communication between the members of a community and the creator thrives. You can learn a lot about the opinions and insights from reading comments under domain experts' videos.

People subscribe to those creators' channels, access their (often thematically organized) playlists. They sign up for notifications and get emails when new videos are released. Since video production is wildly more complicated than writing a tweet or taking a photo, content is released less often but has much higher engagement when it's published. Subscribe to the right channels, and creators will reliably deliver new developments in any industry into your email inbox.

Since watching videos costs viewers a lot of time, the quality expectations for content are quite high. You can expect that niche content with lots of positive engagement is useful and insightful. Creators who try to game the system might succeed when they have a regular influx of thousands, if not millions, of new subscribers. Niche creators have to build real relationships with their viewers, though. They will consider which topics will cause new and existing viewers to engage and prioritize accordingly.

Recommendations are a blessing and a curse. When they work in a creator's favor, they will keep their viewers focused on their content for a long time. But once the recommendation algorithm decides to show another channel's video, the original creator is out of luck, and viewers start moving away. In your audience research, try a good mix of following the recommendations and manually searching for another video among the ones provided by a particular creator.

If the creator has tagged their content, search for those tags to find more. Take notes on videos that stand out during your research that you might want to watch for problem discovery later on. Not only will they give you insight into problems and challenges, but they might also be very sharable content for your own audience-building endeavors.

Let's look at our two central questions:

- How can you spot problems and challenges in this community?
- If you are brave enough to read the comments, note when people express strong opinions about problems and solutions in their space.
- Video content takes a lot of time to consume. When videos seem like a drag, watch them at a higher speed or skip through them. Use tools like Otter.ai to transcribe overly long videos so you can screen them in text form.
- What questions should you ask the members of this community?

- "Which channels have the most insightful content for this industry?"
- Reach out to the creator: "What kinds of problems do people often suggest you create videos around?"
- "Where do people who watch these videos usually hang out?"

Online Communities

Social media platforms are focused on relationships between users and consistent cyclical engagement. Traditional online communities form around a medium where anonymous or pseudonymous conversations are tolerated or encouraged. Forums or chat platforms are much more fragmented than social media since there very often is no main activity feed that everyone "should" be engaging with at all times.

In forum-like communities, the subject matter is the main focus of conversations, while on social media, the person talking about something is just as important as the content. For your Embedded Exploration, this means that you will find honest conversations between people who are not trying to establish personal brands. That naturally shifts conversations towards the central focus of the community.

Reddit

Some call it social media; some call it a forum with social media traits. To me, Reddit is a super forum, a community hub. In its groups, called subreddits, communities of all sorts have sprung up. Reddit users, called Redditors, can belong to any number of groups and often cross-post content from one group to another. Beyond that, user-to-user communication is quite limited, and most conversations are held in the publicly visible comments to Reddit posts.

Every subreddit is different. Each has different rules. Those rules are usually expressed very clearly in the sidebar of each subreddit, sometimes in a sticky post as well. Not only will you need to follow those rules once you start engaging with the subreddit community, but they will also give you some insight into the kinds of conversations you can expect — and which topics are not permitted by the moderators. These rules were established as a consequence of community moderation efforts over the years, and they'll show you which topics are particularly prone to causing unrest in the community. While many subreddits employ these rules to combat advertisement, they're a cheap and easy glimpse into that particular community's group psychology.

Most subreddit communities have resource collection threads as a sticky post at the top of their message feed. If you're taking notes and bookmarking links, this will be a treasure trove. Besides actionable content that will allow you to do problem research, you will also find other external communities that you can join. Many Reddit communities have started Slack or Discord instances due to their desire to communicate with each other directly. Just like with Instagram and Pinterest, I recommend following the conversation and joining these chat platforms.

Since most subreddits have a blanket ban on advertising, you won't see much marketing. It will be actively suppressed by the users and the moderation team of those communities. But since every community contains professionals that might have something interesting to show, many subreddits have established a "weekly advertising post," where Redditors can share links and information about their businesses on certain days in a controlled and limited environment. Pay particular attention to those posts: you will learn a lot about problem awareness and solutions ideation in those threads. You can also learn the jargon used for in-group marketing here very efficiently.

Most subreddits link to related subreddits in their sidebar, which makes finding the whole network of any particular community quite easy: find the biggest subreddit, subscribe to that, then find all linked subreddits, check them all out, and join the ones that seem worth it. Repeat this until you can't find any more related communities.

There are several tools that you can use to discover and analyze particular subreddits:

- Subreddit Stats will show you overall trends as well as individual subreddit stats, including most active Redditors and best-performing submissions.
- There even is a subreddit where Redditors will help you find another subreddit[7].
- You can find Reddit-wide metrics on Frontpagemetrics — this tool even allows you to download a full list of all subreddits on the platform.
- Redditlist allows searching subreddits by name and category.
- The visual tool sayit will show you a graph of how subreddits are connected.

Quora

The question-and-answer platform Quora is a gold mine for Embedded Exploration. In the best case, you can quite literally ask the questions you want your target audience to answer, and those of them who frequent Quora will answer them for you. But even just as a research archive, Quora is incredibly useful.

You can search for past questions about the subject matter most relevant for your niche audience. From there, I recommend following the most prolific responders and investigate what other questions they may have answered in the past. In aggregate, these questions will show you the problem spaces of any particular industry or group.

Quora organizes related questions in so-called Spaces. Following these topics will show new and relevant older questions in your Quora feed. Within those Spaces, you can find interesting discussions as well as the people involved in them. Quora users who frequently engage in answering questions are very interesting prospects for direct communication attempts: a person who likes to answer questions will likely agree to be interviewed as a subject matter expert.

Slack

Back in the early 2000s, the Internet Relay Chat (IRC) was all the rage among early internet users. This network consisted of dead simple chat servers with separate chat rooms, all accessible through a standardized protocol, which led to tools like mIRC and Irssi becoming a staple in any budding developer's system. It was a cool way to connect with others, but it required a certain amount of technical skill.

Slack removed that barrier. They created a friendly, usable, highly integrated platform where communities could quickly spin up their own chat environments, with channels, groups, direct messaging, and everything that a modern chat platform needs. Slack grew up to be what IRC made its early users dream of. Slack brought a reliable mix of asynchronous and synchronous communication to the digital workplace.

But Slack isn't used for professional purposes alone. Since everyone can spin up a free Slack instance for whatever purpose, many online communities have moved their communication nexus into such a Slack instance. You will find open-source projects, programming language communities, role-playing gamers, mental health advocates: they have all found a way to have their community members sign up with Slack.

For audience research benefits, Slack is a great place to "just hang out." Since it's a chat platform, you will read about the just-in-time discussion about problems that are immediately felt by your audience. Slack offers message "threads," which, when used, allow people to dive deeply into a conversation without polluting the main chat feed. It's in those threads that you can find and engage with the people who are struggling with something. Reach out to those people either directly in response to their chat messages or open a Direct Message and ask for details there.

Many Slack instances are invite-only. There are, however, automated invite pages that you will be redirected to once you ask people involved in those communities. You might also find a link to this invite page on community wikis or websites. It definitely is worth asking your target audience on social media if there are any Slack communities they can suggest.

Generally, a lot of public Slack instances are searchable in Slack community directories:

- With Slofile, you can search by keyword, category, language, and region.
- There is also a curated list of 2,000 Slack groups and communities.

Most of those Slack instances come with a freemium product's limitations: only the last 10,000 messages are retained. When you find an interesting piece of information, make sure you take a screenshot to archive that data quickly. It might be gone a few days later, depending on the activity levels in that Slack instance.

Generally, I find Slack a great place to learn more about the actual people in a community. Unlike public social media conversations, Slack users will speak more candidly, as they are among other in-group members. As with almost all other communities, this means that you'll get into trouble for overt salesmanship or marketing. Chat platforms are built for people, not brands.

Expect to be booted off any chat platform if people suspect you to be a corporate infiltrator. The antidote is to build genuine relationships with people on the Slack instance. Interact with them when they talk about their problems, engage with their messages, and become a community member.

Discord

While Slack is considered to be the chat platform for professional teams, Discord originated in a more recreational space: online gaming. As a consequence, Discord is focused on providing an enjoyable experience for small groups of highly engaged users, both through a text-based chat system and through real-time voice chat.

Discord isn't for gamers only, though. You'll find communities of university students, religious groups, and musicians.

You can discover publicly listed Discord Servers here:

- Discord Servers
- DISBOARD has a public list of hundreds of thousands of Discord Servers

Many influencers from larger social media sites opened up Discord Servers to have a place to talk to their followers outside of the confines of a centralized social media platform. Just like with Slack, it's a good idea to ask within the social media community if there are any decently populated Discord Servers around.

LinkedIn

Built as *the* professional social network, LinkedIn is beneficial for aspiring entrepreneurs. Not only will you get to connect with influential people in the businesses you might eventually sell your product to, but LinkedIn is also an excellent resource for problem discovery.

LinkedIn offers groups where professionals from one particular field can congregate. To join them, you will need to request access. Ensuring that you're there to adhere to the rules and learn more about the industry will make this easier. These groups are the perfect place to search for problems or ask clarification questions that invite engagement. They're also a great initial hunting ground for interesting connections.

Connect with the major professionals in your target audience, and you will be exposed to the content they share and the conversations they participate in. It's like a metal detector: the well-connected LinkedIn accounts you follow will point you to the most current problems and points of contention in their industries. You can follow hashtags which — unlike on Twitter — are being used deliberately to segment content by topic. This will allow you to find new and interesting connections.

Start with the titans of industry. Connect with them or follow them, and follow their connections or followers who are both the most engaged and have something meaningful to say. Try to avoid connecting with people who are only on LinkedIn to recruit new employees. Not only will recruiter messages start filling up your notifications, but recruiters will also be quite unlikely to engage in conversations beyond their job. Unless your target audience is recruiters (or is heavily reliant on recruiters), try to avoid them.

LinkedIn being a professional network gives you the excellent opportunity to watch how other businesses create leads. By just observing what content gets created and how people interact with it, you will learn a lot about how people communicate in that particular industry. Take note of any professional jargon that you come across.

Online Forums

Before social media, the web was full of self-hosted communities. Call them forums, bulletin boards, message boards; what unites them all is that they are web applications managing user-generated content, with different approaches to hierarchy among their users. Some forums have extremely flat hierarchies and are open to the general public, while others are very exclusive and highly stratified.

Since web forums were the modernized version of newsgroups and mailing lists, they are often quite topical. The more general forums have lost their appeal now that social media platforms have established the one-size-fits-all community model. But niche forums are still widely used by professionals and amateurs alike.

Usually, you can find those forums by googling for things like "Plumbing advice forum" or "tax lawyer web forum." Among the first few dozen search results, you will find forum communities. Since many of those self-hosted communities are quite old (in internet terms), they'll rank quite well on search indices.

Interacting on most forums might require you to register a free account. In some cases, you might need to be approved by the forum moderators, too. Just like with joining Facebook and LinkedIn groups, be clear about your entrepreneurial intentions while making it clear that you're not looking for a sales channel only.

For observational purposes, many web forums don't need to be logged into. You can very likely browse the conversations without having an account on the forum. I still recommend signing up for one, as this will allow you to message other forum members eventually. Make sure the forum policies permit this. Some communities are quick to ban you from their forums if your communication attempts come across as too spammy. Forums come from a time of conversational equality. It's fine to stand out, but acting against the group's interests will get you removed from forums very quickly. Build relationships, engage with other forum members, and you'll find a great place to learn about their issues.

Sometimes, finding web forums is surprisingly hard, as Google might be overwhelmed with SEO-optimized blogs and content sites, making less well-structured forum pages invisible. If you are already engaging with your community on another platform, reach out and ask if anyone knows any helpful web forums. Established community members usually have a good grasp on which forums are alive and which ones have been abandoned.

When analyzing a forum, take particular note of the sticky posts and old threads with high engagement. You will find information akin to an industry history book: what problems do people regularly have, what problems did they have in the past, how did they solve them back then, and how do they do it now?

Take Ravelry, a website for knitters, crocheters, and anyone who likes yarn and patterns. This is a very specific group of people, a niche activity for a niche audience — yet there are millions of patterns for millions of people who frequent the site. The forum started in 2007, and you can find threads (hah!) going back to that date. The forum is fully searchable. Let's say you want to serve the Do-It-Yourself knitting community. There are over two million mentions of the word "problem" on this forum. Two million opportunities for you to research, solve, and find a way to help that community meaningfully. A cursory glance at those search results yields many knitters who'd love to have more insight into the washability of certain yarns, many who are overwhelmed with all the pattern choices and are asking for curation, and some who'd love to know how certain yarn colors look under certain lighting conditions. Even if you are not a yarn person, it's not too hard to imagine that an info product or two could help these people out.

Podcasts

Podcasts are not just audio content that people consume. Behind every successful podcast is a community of listeners that regularly tunes in and reports back. As a podcast host myself, I get comments and suggestions for my show all the time. Listeners are involved, because unlike the faceless radio hosts of a bygone era, podcasters are personal brands that operate purely on their own. These are real people that you can reach out to. People who might talk about your problems or ideas on their show because they find them interesting.

Most podcasts are niche shows. The host is an expert or an enthusiastic learner in one particular field. Be it software development, solopreneurship, trading card games, or naval history: there are hundreds of shows with great hosts and extremely knowledgeable guests.

Interview-based podcast archives are the who's who of any community. Every episode, there is a new guest with a fresh story and a unique perspective. If you want to find a list of whom to follow on social media, comb through the guest names of a few shows in your field and follow every person. Most podcasts put social media links into their show notes.

A podcast host is a community nexus: they know many influential people, as they have had them on their show and built relationships over time. Hosts are also always looking for new and inspiring stories in their field. Reach out via email or on their preferred social media platform, let them know what you're working on. Building a relationship with someone involved in your audience community on a weekly basis is a valuable thing to do. Not only will you have access to someone who has a lot of unique insight into the industry, but you might be interesting interview material for them eventually, which will be very useful once you grow your own following.

Current podcast episodes will expose you to the most recent events in the industry. Most podcast guests talk about the things they are familiar with, but they will always have opinions on controversial things in their field. In interview shows, these topics will eventually come up, and in addition to learning about what they know, you'll hear about how they think.

Podcast hosts pick their guests based on how much they think their readers might love to hear them chat. Consider this feedback mechanism to be a glimpse into the collective psychology of the niche audience that listens enthusiastically to the podcast.

Let's look at our two central questions and how they relate to podcasts:

- How can you spot problems and challenges in this community?
- Listen to the most recent episodes. Figure out which challenges and problems are commonly addressed by multiple guests.
- Search social media for comments on episodes that are relevant to your research. What do people consider important enough to comment on?
- Find common conversation topics across multiple podcast shows in the same industry. Explore the problem spaces around those most commonly occurring topics.
- What questions should you ask the members of this community?

- Ask the podcast host, "Who do you think is the absolute expert to talk to about problem X?"
- Ask the podcast host, "Where does the community who listens to your show hang out?"
- Ask the community, "What's the most insightful episode of this show for someone who is interested in X?"

Private Online Communities

Many of the groups and forums we looked at so far exist in the public space and are comparatively easy to find. Some are entirely off the radar. This means that you won't find them immediately when you start your Embedded Exploration efforts. You'll run into them once you start listening closely to your community. The private nature of those often small and dense groups means that you'll need to be considered a value-adding member of that community before you get invited.

We'll be talking about strategies and methods to become a recognized expert contributor in your community later. At this point, the best course of action is to keep an ear out for private Telegram groups, unlisted Facebook groups, invite-only online forums, and password-protected chat servers. Take a note, learn about the requirements to join, and check if the effort required to do so is worth your time. Some of these communities are extremely specific and require a lot of participation by their members. For observational purposes, that might be more work than you can handle.

When it comes to the quality of research, closely observing a private community from within can yield incredibly insightful results — at the cost of a lot of reputation-building and expected interaction. Unless you know you can handle this right from the start, look for public communities first. They will make it easier to learn more about the community and gradually build expertise.

The best way to quickly find closed communities is to reach out to well-connected subject matter experts with whom you have already built a relationship. People won't tell you where they exchange their trade secrets with each other if they don't know you. But once you have built a genuine connection with a person and they trust you, they are very likely to show you where you can find like-minded people and closed communities.

Offline-First Communities

Let's step back into the physical world for a second. Before the internet took over everything, people interacted in communities just the same. They may not have resembled their digital counterparts, but professional exchange in purpose-aligned groups was alive and well in the purely analog world.

Many of these communities have transitioned at least partially into the digital realm. While many entrepreneurs are very quick to embed themselves in online communities, you should not neglect the offline ones. Decades, if not centuries, of experience are stashed away in old meeting notes, live on in face-to-face conversations between members of those communities, and have not been transferred to the digital platforms.

Sounds old-timey? It's really not. Consider meetups: while they are often organized on the internet, they happen in physical locations to allow people to meet each other. Offline communities are wonderful for building real relationships with people who care about a subject matter. Since these communities organize around events in certain locations, you will find a lot of people coming there over and over again. You can catch up, learn about new developments, and be perceived as a person who is willing enough to spend a day or an evening talking about a particular niche subject.

Let's take a look at the kinds of offline-first communities you can expect to find, where they are, what events they might offer, and how to embed yourself in them.

Formal Communities

Most offline communities are "official" in some way: they're registered somewhere, they have leadership, they have formalized rules and codes of conduct. That makes them easy to find. Wherever something is registered with a government agency, there will be an official directory. Even for private communities, you can expect these directories to exist within the larger industries and fields of interest in which they exist.

Professional Associations

Any trade or profession needs to organize. It might be to set industry-wide standards, to coordinate working with legislators, or to simplify complicated logistics within a field. These organizations most often form around a common practice. Additionally, they are often restricted to a particular location, as operating within multiple legislative environments is quite complicated. That's why there is a National Farmers Union in Canada and a National Farmers Union in the United States of America. They might cooperate, but they are not the same.

Trade associations, guilds, and unions are the most important organizations for audience exploration purposes in professional fields.

Professional associations often are organized in hierarchical structures mirroring the geographical makeup of who they represent: federal associations have state chapters, and within those state chapters, city chapters, and other kinds of local chapters.

This is great for you in a few ways. First, you can find association members near you that you can meet in person for interview purposes. Since organizations keep detailed member lists for reporting and tax purposes, asking for contacts will very likely yield several people you can quickly connect with in your area. Also, talking to organization administrators at different levels will give you insight into the distribution of problems and challenges across the distinct geographical layers: while some local chapters might often run into legal issues, others in different jurisdictions might not. You can only learn about this by asking someone who has the birds-eye perspective on such information.

All professional associations are active communities with varying degrees of bidirectional communication. At the very least, the administration sends a newsletter every now and then. In the best kinds of communities, a private forum is used by many members on a daily basis. The best way to get access to these resources is to be an actual member of the association. This might be hard for trade associations as they might require you to be an actual member of the trade. Alternatively, you can try to find a trade member to forward you this information or to communicate on your behalf. That's why it's so important to consider who you have access to in your circle of family and friends when you go through the initial audience discovery steps.

Communication channels in associations aren't limited to newsletters. You'll find that some groups publish print magazines (which are also distributed digitally in many cases) that contain not only the latest from their field but also provide an excellent opportunity to learn who is advertising to this audience and what jargon they use. Getting your hands on these publications should be your primary focus from the start. Many magazines also include contact information for local chapters — a gold mine if you're looking for people to interview.

Not all associations are focused on a professional industry. Many hobby associations are taking their community and their impact on their fields just as seriously. Consider FIDE, the International Chess Federation. Not only do they organize professional tournaments, but they track the individual ratings of every registered player — and there are millions of chess players — and work tirelessly to promote the sport and make it more accessible. Such an association's organizational scale can be intimidating, and there will be a lot of information to sift through. Never forget that the whole point of these groups is to make things better for their members. If you reach out to an association and make it very clear that you're trying to understand and help their members, you will get a positive response. Your goals and their goals are very much in alignment.

Let's look at our two central questions and how we can approach answering them for professional associations:

- How can you spot problems and challenges in this community?
- Find the publications and communication nexus of every association. What is being discussed? What are people looking for help with?
- Find out which events you can attend to learn more about the day-to-day problems of the community members.
- Explore the structure of the organizations and reach out to members on different levels with the same questions. Observe the different kinds of focus you'll find in their replies.
- If multiple associations exist within the same space: why are there so many? How do they differ? Do they

serve different audiences, or do they serve the same audience differently?

- What questions should you ask the members of this community?
- "Who in this organization can help me find the experts I need to learn more about X?"
- "Is problem X commonly felt by everyone in your community? If not, do you know what impacts this perception?"
- "Are there problems that only occur for a specific subset of this community?"
- "What institutional roadblocks do you wish would evaporate immediately?"

Clubs

On a smaller scale, you'll find clubs and societies. While they are often organized under the umbrella of an association, they are more self-contained localized communities. It's the difference between a local chess club and the International Chess Federation. Local clubs are more down-to-earth, focused on small-scale events and building relationships with sponsors and donors in the local economy. There is no better place to learn of the real problems experienced by your target audience than joining them talking about their issues in these small-scale groups.

Usually, people organize their gatherings by being at the same place simultaneously on certain days in any given month. These recurring events still happen for many clubs. Chess practice every Wednesday at an Italian restaurant. Book club meeting every second Friday of the month in the library. A startup pitch competition at the local accelerator every other Wednesday. All of these meetings provide opportunities to meet your target audience face-to-face. You'll meet the subject matter experts, often on panels or at least leading the conversations. You'll also meet novices, new members of the community, and even people who are just interested observers like you. Every single person is a source of information about what moves them, what issues they have, and how they can be helped — by you.

Here are a few ideas to answer our two central questions:

- How can you spot problems and challenges in this community?
- Learn from people face-to-face. Ask them about their work, their interests, their challenges. Listen to conversations and take note of topics that come up over and over again.
- Look for the classifieds. Some clubs have boards, analog or digital, where members can ask other members for things or services they need.
- What questions should you ask the members of this community?
- "Who of all the club members you know personally is the de facto expert when it comes to X? Any chance you could introduce me?"
- "What have you done to try and solve problem X? Who told you about that solution? Is anyone else you know suffering from the issue?"

Conferences and Shows

Meetups are nice and cozy, often just held for a handful of people. But their bigger cousin, the conference, is a significant research opportunity as well. Trade shows, summits, and conferences are annual events that bring together large crowds of enthusiastic industry members. Things are being taught, sold, negotiated, and released during these events. At every conference that I have been to, I have met new and interesting people who have taught me something new or with whom I have built a business relationship that has taken me to a new level.

For research purposes, visiting a conference with an open mind and a notepad is like walking into an event that was tailor-made for audience research. You'll find insights on many levels:

- **Look at who is attending the conference: vendors, speakers, sponsors, visitors.** This is the lay of the land for a whole industry. New players join the fray every year, and comparing attendance over the years will show you who joined — and, even more important, who isn't around anymore.
- **Geography matters:** big players have bigger representation; smaller and newer ones usually are co-located. You can learn a lot about the relationships between competitors by just looking at the exhibition hall floor plan.
- **Topics and tracks:** conferences are the medium of collecting learning for industries. The things discussed on stage are the most relevant current problems that the industry is facing and which solutions have been proven to work. For multi-track conferences, consider each track topic a viable sub-niche of the initial audience, with their own problems and challenges.
- **The hidden hierarchy of panels:** on-stage discussions allow you to understand who the key people are in any given industry — who are the established players, who is up-and-coming, and who is considered moderator material. Each of those roles has a slightly different perspective. Reach out to all those people with the same question, and you will get

a nuanced answer that might be different in crucial points.

- **Social networking events:** learn who invites people to those mixers and lunches. These are the community assemblers, great people to talk to to get recommendations and introductions.
- **Publications:** lots of conferences publish some sort of magazine before, during, or after the conference. This will allow you to prepare for the actual event just as much as it will be a source of follow-up contacts for your in-depth interview efforts after the conference.
- **The hallway track:** many interesting conversations happen between conference visitors outside of the scheduled programming. Where groups of people mingle, information is exchanged. Hang out with people, ask them about what they are doing, and learn about what drives them. People will often tell you about their projects, which will allow you to get a glimpse into the problem space as they see it.

Conferences can be quite costly to attend. While you can always consider this an educational expense, it might be prohibitive. You can still gather a lot of information from the schedules and informational materials that are available online. Reach out to the conference organizers to see if they can email you any publications. You might even get free tickets or severely reduced rates. You just have to ask.

Many conferences are also live-streamed or offer an archive of recorded talks and panels once the conference is over. Sometimes this will cost you a fee, or it might be freely available on YouTube. In any case, this is not only a good way to re-live a conference you visited, but it also gives you access to the main content of those events you didn't get to be a part of, including past year's events.

Let's answer our two central questions:

- How can you spot problems and challenges in this community?
- Observe the relationships between participants. Who are the big players, who are the underdogs? Who shows up for every conference in the field, and who was once omnipresent but has vanished? This will show you shifts in the problem space.
- Listen to attendees. Many conference visitors have clear problems that they need to be solved, which is why they come to conferences in the first place. Take notes after each conversation.
- Look at the topics that made it into the talks and panels of the conference you're attending. Are there common themes? Are there different tracks that indicate different sub-niches in the industry? What do they have in common, and where do they differ?
- What questions should you ask the members of this community?
- "Who should I talk to, right here, right now, if I want to learn about the most pressing problems of the industry?"
- "Which problems of this industry are not being solved sufficiently by the vendors that are present here today?"
- "What do you think people should talk about more?"

Other Forms of Communities

There are countless communities out there that don't fit the categories I have laid out here so far. Here's a list of the kinds of communities I have not touched on:

- Professional networks
- Newsletter platforms and communities
- Lobby groups
- Mastermind groups
- Artist collectives
- Blogs and syndication networks
- Sports leagues and associations
- Learning groups
- Genealogy-focused and historical societies
- Reading groups and circles
- Language learning exchange networks

If you're interested in learning and embedding yourself in any kind of community, focus on these principles:

- **Reach out with intent and honesty.** Any community with a common goal will support those who are willing to help them. Truthfully explain why you're reaching out, what your goal is, and how you would like to involve them.
- **Don't skip a community because it's hard to research.** Spend some time learning about the people involved and build cursory relationships. Present yourself as the curious person that you are.
- **First, listen. Then engage.** Jumping into a community and throwing insights at people will cause people to dismiss you as yet another spammy marketer. Observe and understand how people in this community talk and what they care about. Then, slowly, engage by participating in conversations. You'll be able to set the tone later. Understand that particularly in the beginning, this is not about you, but about them.
- **Do recursive community exploration.** In any given

community, find the other community platforms where people congregate. Make a list, or draw a network graph, to see how communities are connected.

- **Ask around at the nexus.** Find the most well-connected people in the field, build a relationship with them, and expand your search for experts and other communities from there.

OFFLINE EVENTS DURING A GLOBAL PANDEMIC

Global pandemics have always impacted the way humans interact. The Spanish Flu pandemic of 1918 wiped out so many people that workers were in such high demand that they could force progress in health care, wages, and working conditions[1]. Unions started forming, and strikes proved to be a worthy method of demanding change.

The COVID-19 pandemic impacted the way communities interact. Social distancing and a general unease about being in close proximity to other humans have affected many offline communities: either they have moved online or have severely changed their approach to how they were conducted. Long-standing events have struggled to maintain their cadence, some have perished completely, and new ones have shifted to a digital model.

So when it comes to conferences and meetups, you'll need to follow the community. If in-person conferences move online, move your research online as well. Instead of talking to people in conference center hallways, reach out to them in the Slack channels or visitor-only forums that the conference organizers set up. It won't be the same, but it doesn't have to be. Consider that the event's purpose is still the same: people are looking for connection and are willing to learn.

Events that occurred in a physical space regularly before they were quickly moved into the digital realm often suffer from the setback of invalidated experience: what worked well before for a physical gathering might not be the right choice for a virtual event. Try getting a show-of-hands for a virtual audience that won't even show their faces. Expect this to be a transitionary state. While some communities may find new homes in the digital space, many will want to — and might need to — get back to (at least partially) physical-space events.

Consider that you can always reach out to the people who used to hold these events before the pandemic and ask them how you can facilitate and support their continuation. From the start, consider becoming a pillar of support for any distraught community you encounter. In the long run, this will provide you with relationships and insights — and maybe a few friendships along the way. Be kind, especially in trying times.

HOW TO TAKE NOTES IN COMMUNITIES

When I do audience research, I try to keep some sort of structure to my notes. Whenever I find something insightful or thought-provoking, I try to note it down in a specific way.

For everything worth writing down, I try to provide Reason, Detail, Context, and Followup.

- **Reason:** Why did I find this outstandingly interesting? What makes this helpful or instructive in understanding my audience better?
- **Detail:** Since whatever I note down will likely be part of a conversation, what is the exact content I am interested in? Can I provide a link or screenshot for later research?
- **Context:** And since this Detail occurs in a larger conversation, what was the initial trigger? Is the soundbite I picked representative of the general opinion? Is it contrarian? Who is the person that said this?
- **Followup:** What can I learn from this? Is there a chance that reaching out to the person who said this

might teach me more? Where do I go to follow up? (Usually, a social media profile or email address is enough for this.)

I am aware that note-taking[1] is a very personal matter. There are note-taking communities[2] that care exclusively about finding the right way to jot down insights. Find a way for your notes to make sense to you.

PRESENTING YOURSELF TO THE COMMUNITY

First impressions matter. When someone checks out your social media profile, and they see a picture of a real human being that's accompanied by a meaningful description and a few well-selected links, they will be intrigued by who you are and what you're trying to accomplish. If they find a default avatar picture and a half-assed description, they'll quickly move away from your profile.

When you're new in a community, people expect some level of initial effort after you join. Make it easy for people to get to know you. The real you. Don't hide behind a pseudonym. Own your name and use it for your public work. Some communities might allow pseudonyms, but the chances are high that members expect you to show your face and use your name if you're in a professional community.

That means that your avatar picture should always be a picture of yourself. It doesn't have to be the suit-and-tie kind of professional photo. Use an image that shows the real you, a person that other people would want to interact with. You expect to be able to talk to real people in the communities you embed yourself in. Return the favor and be a real person for them to engage with.

When it comes to your bio or description, I have found it's best to share what you like to talk about. If you're interested in helping marketers become more effective, say that. If you have 20 aquariums at home, share that with the world. Talk about what you care most about and give community members a sense of the many facets of your life. People appreciate when their peers are entrepreneurial and interested in supporting their community.

So far, the best Twitter bio I have come up with for myself is:

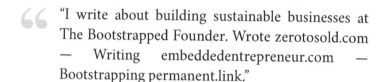

"I write about building sustainable businesses at The Bootstrapped Founder. Wrote zerotosold.com — Writing embeddedentrepreneur.com — Bootstrapping permanent.link."

Anyone who visits my Twitter profile learns immediately what I'll be talking about. If they're interested in what I work on, the links will take them there. Imitation works well in most communities: investigate how thought leaders and influencers present themselves and find a similar way to do it yourself.

The point of all these little things is to give a great first impression. If you send someone a message and they don't know you, this is incredibly important. If they don't find sufficient information about your trustworthiness within a few seconds, they will ignore you — or worse, report you for spam or similarly abusive behavior. What they find in your profile needs to make them curious about you. It needs to want them to build a relationship with you.

This will be slightly different for each community you join. You'll want to talk about your aquarium-related preferences more in a forum for fish lovers, and you'll likely omit this particular hobby when you're embedding yourself in a completely unrelated community. Just avoid being one-dimensional.

TRACKING INFLUENTIAL PEOPLE
ACROSS PLATFORMS

You can significantly speed up the recursive search for communities within communities if you research the most influential accounts. Many thought leaders and industry experts who have a popular account on one social media platform will likely have accounts on other platforms as well. Many notable LinkedIn accounts have a Twitter presence, and many Instagram influencers are active on Facebook or YouTube.

If you find a domain expert you really like, try finding their other social media accounts, follow them there, and start exploring the followings and communities in which they are active. The influencer will often provide slightly different content to their audience on different platforms, which is instructive for understanding what expectations people have in different communities. Additionally, going to another platform will expose you to new accounts that are only active in that particular medium.

Many outstanding community members focus on one or two main communities. Some have understood the flywheel effect of cross-linking communities, while others are purists for one reason or another. Always explore where a single influential account might lead you. They know the lay of the land better than anyone else, and you'll benefit from following them wherever they go to connect with their peers.

THE CARDINAL RULE OF EMBEDDED
EXPLORATION: DWELL, DON'T SELL

Communities are tribal; they are based on honesty and reputation. You'll get away with certain things in one community that will get you removed from others, but the general rule of every community is this:

Every action taken by a member of the group should benefit all members of the group.

This rule is the simplest version of these variations that you'll find in the wild:

- **"Don't critique others' work without productive feedback."** — If you tear down something, provide the means for people to improve.
- **"All posts should be related to X and should be a question. All other posts will be removed."** — This question-centric community had terrible experiences with people just writing opinion pieces. Every post should be a learning and a teaching opportunity.
- **"No personal attacks — criticism of ideas is allowed, attacking people is not."** — At the end of the

day, a community is only as strong as the bond between its members.

- **"No self-promotion."** — The most common variant. Don't make a post about yourself. Don't sell something that primarily benefits you. This is the rule you should pay the most attention to.

All communities have rules. Members are expected to follow these rules, and exceptions are rare. If you don't have a reputation, people will look at you as an outsider, a potential source of trouble. Your actions will be scrutinized particularly strongly, and any deviation will be dealt with much faster and stronger than if a long-time community member were to act in the same way.

Generally, every community is wary of unexpected advertisements. Over time, any group of people will be visited by a marketer, and they will unleash their marketing copy on their "waiting audience." If this happens enough times, the community administration will take steps to prevent this from happening again.

During your Embedded Exploration, refrain from posting content that could be considered marketing. You have joined this community to learn and observe. There is a time and a place for promotion, but it is not now.

"Dwell, don't sell" means being part of a conversation without making it about your product. You want to be recognized as a domain expert over time. Note how this is a passive phrase: you're being recognized by others. It's not you "getting something done." It happens because other community members make a choice. The more you make your interactions about them, the faster they will see you as a valued contributor.

There is a not-so-subtle difference between sharing a few paragraphs that contain a link to a blog post on your company website (good) and sharing just a link to a landing page for your product (bad). Both pieces of content get people onto your page. But only one of them is acceptable in many communities. Just sift through the last few dozen posts or pieces of content in your community. Note the ones that are mentioning products or services and how directly they do it. Try to be even more nuanced in your content.

Let me give you an example scenario. Let's say we're on the /r/Entrepreneur subreddit, a community with a very strict no-advertisements policy. Not only are they very strict about this, but they also have a keen sense of detecting hidden marketing. After all, this subreddit is visited by hundreds of thousands of entrepreneurs. Everything has been tried before.

You want to share your SaaS project idea with this community. Let's say you're interested in building a tool for entrepreneurs to handle international sales tax collection. You have found this to be a problem for a lot of European founders in particular. You have come up with a clever workflow that might make this a lot less confusing. Now you need input on your solution.

Here is what you *shouldn't* write:

"Hey guys, I am *X*, the founder of *Y*. I need to validate my SaaS idea. European founders, please head over to *Y*.com and fill out my 400-question survey. You'll get the first few months of my SaaS *Y* for free when it launches."

Note how this isn't even really an ad. It's just a very blatant attempt to pull people out of their community to benefit your personal agenda. It's trying to sell them on filling out your survey for free, with the vague promise of some future benefits. You're providing no value to the community at this point, but you ask them to come to your aid.

You'd be surprised how many of these posts get written and quickly taken down in this subreddit. Thankfully, your posts don't have to look like this.

Instead, try something along these lines:

"Hey everyone, I am *X*, and I am currently researching international sales tax since I ran into this issue in my professional job as a *Y*, and I think this needs to be solved better. I've been talking to a few founders recently, and here are my learnings:

- Founder *A* from *B* mentioned that...
- I learned talking to an agency in *C* that for them, this problem occurs very often...
- ...

I am still collecting insights from people who have trouble with this issue. Please comment below or send me a DM. I'll keep this post updated with any new piece of insight I can find.

Since I talked to a few tax attorneys along the way, here are a few ideas they had to make this easier for people dealing with this problem right now:

- Option *X*: Use a spreadsheet that does *XYZ*...
- Option *Y*: Follow these four steps every month: ...
- ...

Thank you, everyone, for being part of such a helpful community."

See how this post is providing context, immediate value, and doesn't even need to include a link to your landing page to encourage people to reach out? Even better, you'll establish direct relationships with founders who are eager to find help. You can always throw your survey link at them in a DM, but wouldn't a video call be much better for your validation needs? Don't try to sell them on a product. Sell them on yourself as a person to trust.

The no-advertisements policy extends to free offerings, too. People understand all too well that free products have to monetize somehow, and if users don't pay money, they still generate revenue in some form. That revenue is likely to be used to further a business goal and not the community's goals. Don't try and lure people with free products without providing actual value to the community as itself.

Don't sell. Don't market. Just learn — and share what you learn.

NEXT-LEVEL EMBEDDING: GET A JOB

So far, we have considered Embedded Exploration to be something you do during your free time or as a part-time side-project activity. There is another, albeit much more elaborate, approach to learning something in a field: get a job in it.

Many successful businesses were founded by people who worked in an industry, felt the painful problems themselves, and couldn't help but solve them: first for themselves, and then for others. My friend Steve Lamar, founder of the promotional calendar SaaS PromoPrep, explained to me how working in an agency and seeing their client struggle with coordinating their promotional content was so noticeable and widespread as a problem that he understood its criticality immediately. Now, a few years later, Steve's niche-specific SaaS solution is growing and growing. Working in the marketing field will make you aware of the problems of marketers and their clients.

You don't have to take a full-time job to benefit from this insight. Freelancing, part-time jobs, or even interning will give you access to both the interesting knowledge and the people who hold it. It will allow you to attune your understanding of an industry to the reality of the day-to-day work within it.

One of the most interesting learnings that I had from working as a software engineer in very different industries was to find what I call the "Delay in Technology Transference." For example: in some industries, using shared file storage services like Dropbox is perfectly normal, while in others, people resort to email attachments exclusively, even when no regulation or requirement prevents them from using superior cloud-based solutions. Understanding where something normal in industry A can make a whole lot of difference in industry B becomes much easier when you have spent a few months working for businesses in both of them.

The first-hand experience you can gain from being both a participant and an observer in a community — and this can be a single company just as much as it can be the industry itself — is substantial and will often contain incredibly hard-to-obtain information. At the same time, it is a very large commitment, no matter if you're just freelancing for a project or taking a full-time job. Compared to spending a few minutes on social media every night, taking up a paid gig is something you should only do when you know that there are insights to be gleaned that you wouldn't be able to learn from mere observation.

I consider this an extreme version of Embedded Exploration, but it's worth considering, particularly if you're fed up with your current job anyway. You might as well jump into a new field and see if your prior knowledge and the problem discovery frameworks that we will talk about now will show you the path to an interesting business.

PROBLEM DISCOVERY

FINDING PROBLEMS AS AN
EMBEDDED ENTREPRENEUR

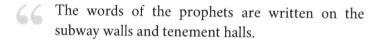 The words of the prophets are written on the subway walls and tenement halls.

PAUL SIMON

The goal of Embedded Exploration is to understand an audience enough to detect how you can help them. You're focusing your attention on becoming an expert in the subject matter, the people, the relationships, and what drives your audience. Now that you have been an active part of your target audience's communities, it should be easy to find their problems and challenges, right?

Well, in reality, communities are messy, chaotic places. Thousands of voices talk about thousands of things, and it's very hard to find the hidden gems among the rubble.

I have found that mental models and checklists are the most helpful things to source problems within a community. Let's look at the inner and outer markings of interesting problems, so you can recognize them better while you're embedded in a community.

The goal of Audience Discovery was to find an audience to serve. During Audience Exploration, you learned how they communicate in their communities. Problem Discovery will focus on discovering the challenges and issues that you can build a business around.

Problem Discovery is over when you have selected a problem to solve and started working on a solution.

PROPERTIES OF AN INTERESTING PROBLEM

First, let's look at what makes a problem interesting enough to note it down in our search for the perfect business opportunity. Different people will define the word "problem" differently. For this book, a "problem" is anything that stands in the way of people accomplishing their goals. If they feel some sort of pain you can relieve, that's a problem. If they have a job that needs to get done or a goal you can help them achieve, that's a problem. Even if you can help them gain more of something than they have now, that's a problem that you can help solve.

Here's the problem with problems: they are something intangible, something that is individually perceived. Every person feels a problem differently.

Consider two people with the exact same job in the same industry. Imagine we're looking at bookkeepers who need to import the monthly sales figures from a SaaS business. One of them feels the problem acutely, having to go through thousands of invoices by hand every month, while the other person has found a makeshift solution using an Excel macro and therefore is only mildly inconvenienced.

Consequentially, only the first person might be looking for a solution. In fact, the same person might perceive any particular problem differently over time, as they put systems in place or experiment with a solution to deal with the challenge.

Since problems are perceived strongly or weakly, we need to look at what happens at either extreme. People don't pay for solutions to problems they don't mind having. If a person doesn't feel pain, they aren't looking for a painkiller. They probably won't even prepare for a time when they might have the pain in the future. But once they feel the pain intensely, they will look for a remedy immediately.

There is the concept of building a product that is a "painkiller instead of a vitamin." Painkillers solve clearly defined problems right here and now, while people take vitamins in the hope that they will prevent potential issues. A painkiller's value is immediately apparent, while a vitamin may or may not provide the intended returns. Still, both painkillers and vitamins sell pretty well, just to different audiences.

Particularly if you are self-funded, this is a critical consideration. Do you want your product to be the main dish, or are you happy with it being the optional side dish? Everyone orders the main dish when they go to a restaurant, but a side dish can find a much better-defined audience. When we build main dishes, we might compete with much better-financed businesses. The moment we go for side dishes, we risk building something that isn't a must-have.

There is no definitive answer to which option you should pick. Founders are successful with both approaches: you can find opportunities to build solid and sustainable businesses either way. So how can we increase our chances of finding a problem that, when solved, will allow us to create a business that enables us to reach our entrepreneurial goals?

I believe that we have a shot at success as long as the

problem we solve is critical. The moment we focus on helping our audience deal with a critical problem, we build something that people actually need because it solves a critical problem.

A critical problem is both important and urgent. It's likely a painkiller, as vitamin-like problems are optional by definition. Solutions to critical problems are "must-have" products. A nice-to-have product solves a non-critical problem.

Before we dive deeper into the properties of such critical problems, it's helpful to understand what kinds of problems you'll encounter in general since criticality is highly dependent on where a problem originated.

The Three Kinds of Problems

Critical and non-critical problems alike fit into one of three categories. They can be:

- **Time-related problems:** "This takes too long. This happens too often." Productivity issues and tedious chores cause pain because they make people feel like they're wasting their time. Whenever people complain about something being inefficient or tedious, you are looking at a time-related problem.
- **Resource-related problems:** "We can't afford this. Too many people are working on this." If you hear people complaining about a waste of money, prohibitive costs, regulatory compliance, or the wrong people working on the wrong things, you're looking at a resource-related problem.
- **Problems of the self:** "This makes us look bad. This prevents us from getting where we want to be." These intrinsic problems are felt on a personal level. Everyone wants to feel accomplished and recognized

by their peers. Anything that touches the fields of Reputation, Accomplishment, Advancement, and Empowerment can be considered an intrinsic problem.

In many ways, you can trace most time- and resource-related problems back to a problem of the self:

- The H&R management software that a company is using may be too expensive, yes. But it's not just about the money. Someone made a choice to buy it. The person who bought it is considered incompetent or wasteful, damaging their professional reputation.
- A regular maintenance task — creating the yearly inventory report — takes a long time to solve, which causes the person responsible for doing it to look lazy and undeserving of a promotion.

Always consider that overtly obvious problems might have a hidden side-effect that causes an intrinsic problem as well.

Most critical problems, therefore, are always partially intrinsic. The good thing is that the problems of the self cause people to act, and that's something we can observe. Whether through Google Search keyword rankings or because someone complains about something on Twitter, critical problems leave a detectable trace.

The Properties of Critical Problems

If you look at a problem and need to figure out if it's critical for the people who experience it, look for as many of the following properties as possible. The more boxes the a problem checks on this list, the more likely it is a strongly felt pain that prospective customers would pay to have solved:

- Critical problems are **painful**. They involve a loss of some sort: the person's quality of life is often severely impacted. Either financially or by wasting time, a critical problem *hurts*.
- You can't ignore critical problems. They cause **real and measurable pain** every time they occur. Not solving them will cause frustration very quickly. Critical problems are non-optional; they can't just be opted out. Often, you can't even delegate them: if you have this problem, you're stuck with it until it is resolved.
- Critical problems are **frequent and recurring**. They are so present in the minds of your audience because they keep coming back. And when they come back, they need to be solved, again and again, every single time with the same level of effort.
- Critical problems take up **non-negligible amounts of time** — every time. You can't solve a critical problem quickly. Deferring the work usually causes even more work in the future. A critical problem will feel like an unwelcome chore: important, yet tiresome.

Because the people in your audience experience critical problems so clearly and can measure the pains and costs attached, they will be very capable of calculating the value of any solution that solves their problems. People gladly pay as soon as paying for the solution is cheaper than continuing with how they attempted to solve their problems before.

As a general rule, people will pay for a solution:

- if it **saves them time**
- if it **saves them money**
- if it **makes them money**

If your solution does all three, you've hit the jackpot. But we're getting ahead of ourselves here. Now that we know what a critical problem looks like, we should look closely at how you can find it within the communities that you're embedded in.

THE SHAPE OF A PROBLEM IN THE WILD

The wonderful thing about humans is that they have a hundred different ways to talk about their dreams, desires, needs, and challenges. No two people will talk about their experiences the same way. Thankfully, we can group these messages into several easy-to-recognize categories.

Here's an important thing to understand: Problem awareness can't be expected by default. Many people walk through their lives, dealing with problems but not recognizing that something is wrong: to them, it's just the way things are. When someone asks for a recommendation, not only have they understood that they have a problem, they have also learned that they can solve it and that there are solutions that others could recommend to them.

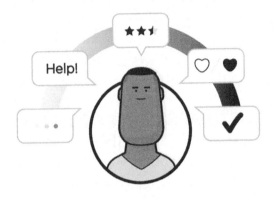

Let me introduce Eugene Schwartz's Prospect Awareness Scale, a handy categorization of different states of clarity about any given problem in their space. Here's a quick rundown of this scale, from lowest awareness to highest:

- **Completely Unaware:** The person is not aware of the problem at all. They are most likely to **complain** about a pain they feel.
- **Problem-Aware:** The person understands they have a problem but is unaware that someone has already solved it. They are most likely to **ask for help**.
- **Solution-Aware:** The person knows that their problem can be solved but doesn't yet know that you offer a product that does. They're most likely to **ask for recommendations**.
- **Product-Aware:** The person knows what you sell but is also looking at the competition. They will **ask for alternatives** to your products or your competitors' products.
- **Most Aware:** The person knows your product and

only needs to be convinced to use it. They're just looking for the right deal. For problem discovery, this group isn't too interesting. Super interesting for any sales activities at some later point, though!

People Start Complaining

This might be the most obvious hint that there is something wrong: people quite literally telling you that something is not working for them. Anything that starts with one of these phrases can be considered a complaint:

- "I can't believe X is so hard…"
- "Why is there no X for Y…"
- "I can't figure out how to X…"
- "How on earth do people deal with X…"

The common theme among complaints is that they usually come after someone has attempted to solve a pressing problem unsuccessfully. Their frustration levels rising, they eventually escalate to sharing their annoyance in their communities.

Understand that a complaint is usually an explosive message. It might draw a bleaker picture than the person would feel in another situation. Still, a complaint is a clear indicator of a pain, a strongly felt one at that. If you see regular complaints about a particular issue, you might be looking at a very critical problem.

When people vent their frustration, consider holding back on the engagement for a bit. A person who just typed furiously to deal with their pain is not the best candidate for a thoughtful and calm conversation. Take a note of the conversation happening and engage a bit later, maybe even through another channel rather than directly responding to the original message or thread.

People are Asking for Help

While complaints are usually very emotionally charged, requests for help tend to be more solemn. Although they're often worded in a similar way, complaints aren't intended to actively seek assistance. Complainers are usually looking for consolation and commiseration. A person asking for help, however, is looking for a more interactive experience.

When people ask for help, they have exhausted their repertoire of solutions. Particularly in professional communities, people will try many things before they consider asking others for assistance. While in certain communities, it's perfectly fine to ask for help, it may be considered a sign of weakness and lack of experience in others. Your Embedded Exploration efforts should have provided you with some insight into this threshold so that you can distinguish how experienced any given person asking for help might be.

By virtue of having limited knowledge, beginners will ask for help faster and more often, which will skew the quantitative distribution of "asking for help" messages towards the novices in any given field. Every now and then, an expert will ask such a question. Pay particular attention to those posts, as they point at critical problems that even the most experienced professionals (who often have interesting budgets) have trouble with.

Take notice of who responds to people asking for help and how they approach both solving their problem and asking for clarification. You will learn a lot about how solutions in this space can be analyzed by observing how people try to find the root causes of problems.

The people who jump at the opportunity to help another community member are the people you want to follow and engage with actively. Consider how much insight they have into the problem space on your target niche: not only do they hang out in the community, they are actively trying to solve people's problems. If there is any person who you should ask about problems they regularly encounter, it would be the person that is always on the lookout for people who need help.

People are Looking for Recommendations

People who don't need help immediately but are interested in preparing for a future problem will trust their community to supply them with valuable recommendations. Whenever people ask for tools, processes, or resources that will help them approach a future challenge with confidence, you should take a note of these things:

- Which products, services, or resources are recommended most often within the replies to this particular question?
- What gets recommended all the time, across many different questions?
- Who recommends these things? How experienced are they? Are they trustworthy? Might they have ulterior motives? How does the community react?
- Is there a follow-up? Does the person who initially asked report back after they have used the recommendation? Did it work for them? (This is a very effective way of evaluating a recommendation. You might even consider asking the requester a few days after they have received the recommendation.)

Try figuring out how the solutions that are being recommended are monetized. This will heavily inform the expectations around price in that community. If every single recommendation is a free tool or resource, you might run into trouble charging for something comparable later.

That doesn't mean a solution to their problem can't be

turned into a viable stream of revenue using other monetization strategies, but I personally prefer to directly charge people money, which directly validates the balance between price and value.

People are Looking for Alternatives

An interesting variation of looking for recommendations is the ever-so-slightly more specific asking for alternatives. Recommendations are open-ended; people take everything they can get. But asking for an alternative is different and much more interesting for the problem discovery process: here is a solution to a validated problem that is not sufficiently solving it. On top of that, someone is actively seeking it.

Since we're very interested in signs of a validated problem, this is a powerful signal. Someone else has found a problem worth solving but has failed to execute the solution. While this means that their solution might need some major tweaks, it pre-validates the problem for you.

The other validation that people asking for alternatives provides is the existence of a budget. Unless the person explicitly asks for free alternatives, you can consider them interested in paying some sort of fee for a solution to their problem. For your future price calculations, it's useful to jot down the average price range of the product for which an alternative is sought. This will give you an anchor price later.

Alternatives also allow you to understand what the workflow of your prospective customers is. Obviously, the product that people want to replace doesn't quite work with how they approach solving their problems. It's a good idea to ask them about this specifically. Since you already know the problem to be valid, this will give you a head-start for invalidating any ideas you might have that will clash with your customers' reality.

Finally, let's look into a few other kinds of messages you might find in communities that are indicative of a problem:

- People are **sharing the (often crude) systems they have made** to solve a problem. Whenever you see someone trying to build an Excel sheet or a Google Doc to enable them to solve an issue, you have found an issue exhibiting several traits of a critical problem: it's recurring and painful enough that someone has built a system around it.

- People are **looking to hire someone** to solve a problem. No matter if they're looking for a contractor for a quick job or a long-term position, this shows that they couldn't deal with a problem and chose to act.

ON BUDGETS AND PURCHASING
AGENCY

Not everyone who has a critical problem will have the means or intent to pay for a solution. Founders often assume that their customers will see the value of a product and pay for it immediately because its value is higher than the price. This is a very theoretical economic perspective, and it ignores the context of many people's lives.

Back when I was a salaried software engineer, whenever I encountered an interesting developer tool that would make my life easier, I had to reach out to my boss to see if we could fit it into our budget. I didn't really understand how flexible our budget was, and I didn't make the purchasing decision. In short, I had no budget insight and no purchasing agency. If the creators of that developer tool marketed the product to me, they would have to rely on me convincing my superiors to buy their tool. So, they usually have a pricing page that is tailored to convince the decision-makers. It also means that they are likely to charge enterprise-level amounts of money.

Now, let's take a look at a completely different kind of audience: freelancers. A freelance software engineer is their own boss. They decide which tools to use; they are a one-person shop. They set a budget for themselves, and they are the ultimate decision-maker. If you want to sell a product to a freelancer, you have to be convincing enough for every single person who uses your product to see the value and consider it both affordable and worth a slice of a limited budget that very likely has to cover household expenses too.

This means that for some people, a critical problem in their professional lives might still not be as important as putting food on the table or paying the mortgage. Consider which expenses your business will be competing with. If possible, move into a market where budgets for such solutions already exist. That's why looking for people asking for recommendations and alternatives is better than just looking for complaints: they are higher up on the Prospect Awareness Scale and need to be educated less about why they should pay for such a solution.

I ran into an interesting situation that I want to warn you about: freelancers who don't see themselves as freelancers. The gig economy has created many positions where people are working in employee-like capacities but are essentially self-employed. When my partner Danielle and I ran FeedbackPanda, an EdTech productivity SaaS for Online Teachers, we looked at such an audience. These teachers were working part-time for big Chinese online schools as contractors. Every teacher had to provide their own computer and classroom materials. The schools only supplied the curriculum and video access to the student. It actually took those teachers a while to understand that they were entrepreneurs. Most came from a salaried background, and they expected their employer to take care of any adjacent services they would need. But now, as contractors for those online schools, they all of a sudden had to set a budget for extra tools — and sign up with their personal credit cards.

Carefully observe your target audience for their understanding of who sets the budgets and who makes the ultimate purchasing decisions. These people are the ones you want to talk to if you ever intend to make money. Particularly for first-time founders, it's important to understand the difference between building something cool because "making it is fun" and building a sustainable business on validated assumptions about who will be paying for what kind of solution to their problem.

A WARNING ABOUT VALIDATION

There is no such thing as a surefire way to build a successful business. No amount of validation can give you that assurance.

As entrepreneurs, we are often very sure of our assumptions. After all, that trust in our ideas makes us undertake our journeys, to begin with. We need to believe in the validity of our ideas and plans to take action.

Without a healthy dose of optimism, we'd just take the (supposedly) safe route of employment and never start our own businesses. But here you are, knee-deep in the process of finding an audience to serve so that you can build a business that will catapult you into financial independence.

But it remains a belief, an untested hypothesis, until we consciously choose to validate it. The founder community often talks loudly about the need for validation: "You shouldn't start a business without validating your idea. Validation is the key to success."

This is an incredibly dangerous statement. It suggests that you can actually validate such a fleeting thing as an idea, a solution, or a potential audience. When founders talk about validation, we often engage in wishful thinking. We say that we want to validate an idea, an audience, or a problem, but we hope to find a way to be sure in reality. We hope to discover a guaranteed win — a surefire way to build a successful business.

There is no such thing.

Validation Does Not Mean Guaranteed Success

A business is always a risky undertaking. That's what entrepreneurship is: an undertaking, an attempt to do something new, trying to create something from nothing.

Entrepreneurship involves the risk of failure at all times. You might start with an idea that attracts no attention or might create the wrong product for the right audience. That uncertainty is why we focus so much on trying to validate our assumptions.

But we approach validation the wrong way. We try to find statements, figures, and opinions that agree with our assumptions. We try to make sure that we are right. If we see enough agreement and confirmation, we think we must be doing the right thing, that our theory is correct.

Here's the catch: you cannot prove theories. Even if you find a million reasons you're right, it only requires a single valid counterexample to disprove the whole theory.

Karl Popper, a German philosopher of science, calls this "falsification." A theory has to be falsifiable and cannot be "verified" completely. We can only claim it to be valid because rigorously attempted falsification did not yield any results.

What does that mean in business terms? You can spend weeks or months trying to find people who — maybe — want to buy your product. Or, instead, you could try to find out why people *don't* need it. You can dive into prior attempts by other founders who ventured to solve the same problem and failed. You can build a functional prototype and ask people to try and pay for it. These actions will produce real results compared to the nebulous "feeling of validation" that asking people if they like your idea would create.

The Validation/Invalidation Principle

You're better off trying to quickly invalidate your assumptions than to validate them. Every theory that you can invalidate is one less mistake waiting to happen. If you fail to invalidate a theory, however much you try, then you're left with something useful to work on. Eric Ries, author of *The Lean Startup*, suggests that you should "try to invalidate your riskiest assumption first."

The secret of validation is understanding that you can never be sure. You can only become less uncertain. For an entrepreneur, that is an important distinction, as it impacts how we weigh the risks of our actions. If you knew something was guaranteed, you'd likely skip building safety mechanisms or looking at alternatives.

That is precisely why founders who misunderstand validation still fail even though our validation results are promising. We often mistake promises for assurance, which leads to some form of entrepreneurial tunnel vision. Assumptions that were "validated" that way are not questioned anymore. Products are built on shaky foundations. Businesses crumble because we only looked at "the happy path" but forgot to consider all the things we *don't* want to happen.

Validation through invalidation is like taking a marble block and carving away at it until the statue emerges. Eventually, the statue will emerge. It might just be a different statue than the one you set out to carve.

For the scope of this book, consider any appearance of the word "validation" to mean "something that withstands thorough invalidation."

Applying the Validation/Invalidation Principle

It really helps to understand how we can use this understanding of validation to get results quickly. Two things are essential to successful (in)validation: "leaving the building" and "avoiding the wrong questions."

You can learn everything about your customers without involving them. While you might ascertain a lot about their needs and desires from observation, you can't do that from a safe distance at all times. Sometimes, you'll need to be a part of the conversation to learn from it.

Luckily, "leaving the building" is a figurative term in our

global digital economy. You will very likely only need a web browser, a microphone, and a camera to do all the validation you'll need. In certain industries, an old-fashioned phone might be required, too. We'll dive deeper into this approach in the next chapter.

It is equally fortunate that there is a wonderful resource on how to talk to prospective customers. The book *The Mom Test* by Rob Fitzpatrick was written for the sole purpose of teaching founders how to avoid asking leading questions. It should be recommended reading for any aspiring entrepreneur.

The Mom Test's premise is that if you ask your parents about the validity of your ideas, they are very likely to be encouraging because that is their job as a guardian. They won't give you their honest opinion; they might not even form an unbiased opinion because their offspring is involved. The moment they sense you're looking for approval, they might conflate moral support with truth, and you end up with answers that will lead you straight to failure.

The crux of the problem is that this behavior is not just limited to your parents. People love to show support and encouragement. Even if you ask a stranger if they like your idea, they might give you a positive response, when deep down, they don't think it's a good idea at all. After all, it's just words, and those are cheap.

The solution is to ask the right questions. Instead of asking if your prospective customers like your idea, have them talk about their problems. Don't ask quantitative questions that can be answered with "yes" or "no," but ask qualitative questions instead: "What problems do you encounter when you try to do X?" "Which tools are you using more than Y times a week?" or "How often do you run into problem X while you try to do Y?" Give your prospective customer the opportunity to share their whole story, not just the figures you're interested in. There are treasures to be found in the minds of your prospects. There are many problems that are very real to them that you don't know yet. Give them — and yourself — the opportunity to dive deep into the reality of your target market.

I've written extensively in *Zero to Sold* about which questions you can ask your prospects to find interesting problems. The same goes for validation approaches for any solution you've come up with.

FINDING THE PROBLEM(S) YOU WANT TO SOLVE

The Problem Discovery step is *not* concerned with *solving* a problem. The result you'll want to get to is a deep understanding of one or many critical problems as they are expressed by the members of the communities you're embedded in.

Throughout your Embedded Exploration, you will have run into any number of interesting problems. You'll have noted them down, and now you will need to decide which issue or cluster of challenges you will want to focus on most.

Problem Discovery: Tracking Sheet

⚲ Search

⚲ Problem	⊙ Appeared as	☞ Who had the problem?	📅 Date	✑ Link	☰ Notes
Can't find readers for self-published books	Complaint	https://www.reddit.com/us er/Helpful_Tajada	Apr 28, 2021	https://www.reddit.com/r/sel fpublish/comments/mz5rkj/i _dont_know_what_the_hell _else_to_do_anymore/	They seem to do very little marketing, have not started audience-building.
Disillusioned by slow progress	Complaint	https://www.reddit.com/us er/HarleeWrites	Apr 27, 2021	https://www.reddit.com/r/sel fpublish/comments/mzj95o/ serialized_web_novel_publi shing_looked_alot_more/	No marketing whatsoever.
Layouting a book is hard	Ask for Recommendation	https://www.reddit.com/us er/RJamieLanga	Apr 23, 2021	https://www.reddit.com/r/sel fpublish/comments/mxxs47/ layout_with_indesign_hire_a _layout_editor_or_diy/	They know that InDesign is commonly used, but may not have the skills. They don't seem to know how much to budget for this.
Feeling the need to diversify sales	Request for Alternative	https://www.reddit.com/us er/babamum	Apr 18, 2021	https://www.reddit.com/r/sel fpublish/comments/mta7rg/ next_best_platform_after_a mazon/	Comments are generally pro-Amazon. They're pointing out that this is a marketing problem mostly.

The audience-driven approach values (in)validation over assumptions. That's why you won't dive into building a product at this point just yet.

Precisely *how* to build a workable product that implements a solution for the problem you have chosen is beyond the scope of this book. There are plenty of resources available to guide you from a vague solution idea to a fully featured product.

What matters for an Embedded Entrepreneur is that building a solution to a problem is not a process that should happen in solitude. Just like a standup comedian, you will need to test your ideas in front of an audience. You'll need to iterate and change them, make them better, and expand on them. Feedback and interaction are fundamental components of this process. None of them would be possible without other people.

Building an audience-driven business requires you to build for and with an audience. It's a self-supporting construct: you start by gathering attention around you and your interaction with the community, then you start working on a solution to people's problems, which invites more people to follow your endeavors, and that results in more insights into your audience's problems that drive your product creation efforts.

Now, it's time to learn how you can create that self-sustaining loop.

AUDIENCE-BUILDING

MAKING FRIENDS FOR FUN AND PROFIT

 There's an audience for everything.

DAVY JONES

Once you have found the people you want to serve and empower, and you have zoomed in on a problem space within their lives, you will now both *build an audience* and *build for that audience*. That's the final step of the Audience-Driven approach, and its goal is to construct a sustainable business that allows you to reach financial independence through entrepreneurial success.

I want to stress once more that the "Audience-Driven" approach is not just about gathering followers on social media, but much more than that. In this chapter, we will look into building a following just as much as we will make sure your audience and you benefit from interacting with each other. We will investigate how you can create and derive value from this mutually beneficial relationship with the people you want to serve.

The Audience-Building phase never ends. It's also a slow

process, so strap yourself in to do this for a few months at least to see meaningful results.

You're building (for) an audience to create a sustainable business from an opportunity that you found by embedding yourself in your audience's communities. Your Audience-Building phase doesn't even end when that business ends. The personal brand you'll build will go beyond any particular business you create. This is an ongoing process that produces more value the longer you stick with it.

A PLATFORM OF CHOICE: TWITTER

While most of the strategic insights from this chapter will work for every audience you'll want to build (for), I will restrict the tactical advice to the Twitter platform, as this is what I am most familiar with I've grown my own Twitter following substantially within a short few years, and I am most embedded in this community.

I provide an extensive resource collection for relevant advice and guides for other communication platforms. Wherever possible, I will try to be both pragmatic and general so that you can transfer these learnings to other platforms.

As you have learned in the Audience Exploration part of this book, your audience of choice will determine the platform on which you will build for them. There is an interesting duality to consider here, though: while your ideal target customer may not be actively using Twitter, a considerable portion of founders and indie hackers frequent this platform on a daily basis. If you want to share your learnings, find helpful guidance, and build a brand as an entrepreneur, I recommend using Twitter for your personal growth. If your target audience is on

Twitter, too, all the better. If not, be present inside the founder community nonetheless. It will make all the difference.

THE GOALS OF AUDIENCE-BUILDING

Let's take a closer look at the goals for audience-building. Many people see audience-building as a means to an end: they expect to build a following of people that are just sitting there, waiting to be sold something. The goal of this very limited audience-building approach is to find as many potential sales targets as possible, sell to them, and that's it.

This is a minimal view of audience-building. A lot of people consider the term "audience" in that narrow, classical way. They imagine a stage, and there's a band playing music. This concept of an audience looks at the people attending a concert as something very passive: they're merely listening. They're consumers. The only thing they do is cheer, but there's no interaction beyond that. It's a unidirectional approach: information flows from the band into the audience, they receive it, and they consume it. And while this is true for many creative workers like musicians and artists, we can expect more of a bi-directional kind of communication in the entrepreneurial world.

But building a business is not just about yelling at people to buy something. This approach might work for some people, but

I don't think it should be the perspective we take to build sustainable and meaningful audience-driven businesses.

So what are the goals of audience-building beyond just building a following of passive consumers?

It's important to understand that there are two goals in building an audience. It's not just about your product or business. It is also about you as the entrepreneur behind the project. It's about building a business brand with your name attached to it and building a personal brand that has your business attached to it.

Adam Wathan is well-known in the software developer community, and people associate his name with his Refactoring UI course, the TailwindCSS project, and the successful TailwindUI product. On a global stage, Sir Richard Branson *is* the Virgin Brand. He embodies the company values and lives them: he is fun, adventurous, ambitious, and progressive.

There are many, many faceless corporations out there: gigantic enterprise businesses that build equally faceless audiences for their products. They only need to know that you belong to the target audience, their consumer base, to sell you their product.

Passionate founders that I've met and talked to in the founder community want their audience to be more than just a number in a spreadsheet. When they think about their customers, they want to understand them. They want to understand what drives and motivates the customer beyond just selling them a product. A founder's mission is to solve their audience's problems and make their lives better in a meaningful way. That alone makes audience-building a different endeavor for indie founders.

When we compare our efforts to build an audience as indie founders and indie hackers to the efforts of much larger enterprise businesses, we encounter wildly diverging amounts of entrepreneurial risk. Entrepreneurial risk in our case means that our startups, the businesses that we found, and the ideas that we have might not work out. And while this is not a big problem for an enterprise business (in that when one of their products doesn't work out, they can just create and sell another product), for an indie founder, failing makes a significant and often financially catastrophic difference. Building an audience allows us not to lose everything when we start something new because our previous attempt didn't work out.

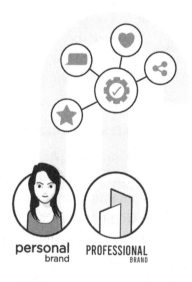

personal brand   PROFESSIONAL BRAND

This is one of the benefits that many indie hackers don't see: when you think about building an audience, you build a personal brand that transcends the business you're starting. Your business is one thing, but you, as a founder, are another equally valuable thing to follow on a social network or within a community. Your expertise, your contributions, and you as a person are all things that your community peers care about.

You still want to make people as interested as possible in the thing you're building, though. It's not just about you as a founder. It's also about what you're doing, how you are helping the community, your chosen audience, with the problems that they have. You want to have your own personal brand as the accomplished founder (or the founder on a journey to accomplishment), and you want to have the brand for your business, the idea, the actual solution to somebody's problem. This is a balancing act, so let's talk about the two main goals that we should follow to get there.

The first goal is becoming a trusted domain expert, and the second goal is building a product that your audience needs.

That's all there is to it: become an expert personally and professionally. Build a product that comes from visible and verifiable needs from within your audience and solves their problem.

The First Goal: Become a Domain Expert in Your Community

Consider where you want to be a year from now. Wouldn't it be great if you had a reputation in your community for knowing what you're talking about? How about lots of people learning from your content, from your posts, and then thanking you in public for your helpful insights?

A recognized domain expert is a person with leverage in the community. This doesn't have to be purely selfish leverage: you can use that leverage for many things for your own success, furthering the success of the community and for eventually elevating other people into positions of success, where you can interact and partner with them and build something more significant.

You won't become a recognized domain expert overnight. This is a long-term play, and it's essential to understand that it is based on trust. Every expert in the community is recognized as an expert because people trust what they have said before. It's really about exposing yourself to a community, sharing your learnings and insights in a meaningful way that helps other people. This, and only this, generates trust.

That trust will, over time, turn into a reputation in the community. Just look at the indie hacker and founder community. The people who are trusted and domain experts in this community, like Justin Jackson, Tyler Tringas, and KP, are trusted because they're consistently providing heaps of value and are earning the trust of their community every single day.

But these people didn't start as experts. They began by being ambitious learners first.

They shared their learning journey, and they never stopped. This made them a trusted domain expert in the end: they started from nothing and had to learn how to learn. Then, they shared their learning journey with other people. They're now recognized as teachers that improve their community.

The Second Goal: Build a Product That Your Audience Needs

Let's take a look at the other side: at the product and your business. Nailing the audience-driven product approach is the second goal of audience-building. Try to achieve the second goal in parallel to your personal journey to domain expertise. Consider this to be an ongoing feedback loop that's at the core of your audience-building process.

Here's the loop: it starts with learning something from your community. Somebody complains about a challenge, or they ask for a recommendation. That's how you learn about an underlying problem, and then you try to validate it. Is it really there? Is this person overreacting, or is there more to this? Are other people complaining about this problem, too?

Based on this, you build something that can solve this for people who have this issue. You release it either just as a concept or as an actual tool. And then, you observe the community's reactions, which will teach you something new, and the loop begins again. You learn, you validate, you build, you release, you observe.

THE THREE PILLARS OF GROWTH

Because you're becoming an expert in your field's challenges and requirements throughout this interaction, this creates personal growth in parallel to your professional growth. There are three fundamental pillars to audience-building growth, which affect your follower count, the quality of your work, and the impact it has on your community.

We're talking about Engagement, Empowerment, and Valuable Content.

It's straightforward:

1. **Engage with people.** Don't just yell into the void.
2. **Empower people.** You can lift them up and multiply the eyes that are on their content.
3. **Provide meaningful, valuable content regularly.**

If you do these things, you will attract people interested in you, your work, and your opinions.

Without this kind of intentional interaction, you would never learn about people's problems. That's why it needs to happen in public. There's a lot of talk about "Building in Public," and I appreciate this because learning, teaching, and feedback are crucial to the entrepreneurial journey. Working in public makes this so much easier.

If you learn in public, other people learn with you. If you teach in public, they learn from you, and you learn from them. A feedback mechanism allows you to better understand people's problems by enabling you to interact with them and see multiple perspectives. As founders, we often believe that we know something. Talk to a few of your prospective customers to see if your world view matches theirs. In many cases, you'll find that your assumptions were highly biased. Only honest and truthful engagement will unearth these secrets for you.

Building (for) an audience in public is extremely valuable because now you're not building an idea-first or a product-first business. You don't just have "a great idea," and you sit there for six months in complete isolation, build it and then throw it on the market. Now, you actually have a consistent validation opportunity when you're engaging with your audience regularly.

THE ABUNDANCE MINDSET

This works so well because founders who build in public work from an abundance mindset. Being involved in a community is an act of abundance, not a zero-sum game. You're not losing anything if you're adding value to something else. Similarly, reaching and teaching as many people as possible is a positive thing. Being exclusive or elitist reduces the potential impact you might have on the lives of others. The abundance mindset is expansive and inclusive.

Consider the whole community to be something that you should support, not just your potential customers. You want to become a person of reputation in your community that others will mention when new members ask whom they should be following.

From a perspective of abundance, competition is not a problem. In a community, you're not even competing with each other. It might feel like you're competing for attention, but even that isn't true. You can share attention. Look at amplifying other people's messages: it's a triple win. It's good for you because you get a tiny fraction of credit for somebody else's tweet. It's fascinating for your followers because they're interested in the things that you share. So that's the second win. The third win is for the person you actually amplify: a person who may have only a few followers benefits massively from having their message syndicated to a much larger audience.

So the abundance mindset shows that the more you can share and amplify within this community, the better it will be for the community as a whole. Particularly on Twitter, where tweets are ephemeral, everybody will get a shot at being seen eventually. Everybody will have their chance.

The abundance mindset also extends to building relationships. Connecting with another person becomes much more enjoyable when you understand that it's not just about an opportunity to sell something but about starting a conversation. When you talk to someone as a peer, you will learn about them and understand them better. They get to know you better, too. If you're interesting, they will start talking about you, introducing who you are and what you are about to other people.

Let's pull all this together: audience-building requires you to build two parallel brands, one for yourself and one for your product and your business. You want people to be interested in what you want to eventually sell and establish a reputation as a caring expert that you can carry with you beyond this particular business. Act from an abundance mindset, engage, empower, and provide valuable content and build in public to leverage the feedback mechanisms that being embedded in a community allows for.

IMPOSTOR SYNDROME AND BUILDING CAPITAL

There will be days when you feel like you have nothing to say. You might wonder why you should be the one talking about anything when there are people out there who are much more experienced than you. You feel like you're acting more knowledgeable than you truly are.

I have been there. Even now, I feel like an impostor, wondering if my understanding of impostor syndrome is worth talking about. Every creator, everyone speaking in public, knows this feeling. It is a part of our brain's wiring to try to protect us from the unknown dangers that we might attract when we put ourselves out there.

Embrace the fear, invite it in, listen to it, and then ignore it. You know what you want, and even if you don't have a clear plan, you know how to get closer to a better, more fulfilled life. Working in public takes courage, and it often is a harder choice to make than just staying silent. But it's always a choice.

Remember this: real impostors don't suffer from impostor syndrome[1]. Growth always involves new and unknown territory, and you will learn how to navigate it.

Understand that by building in public, you are building capital; you're building wealth. Even if you fail or disappoint some people, your struggle and your journey will mean something. People will follow you because of your vulnerability, not despite it. Over time, this shared learning journey and progress will build a following that will be there when you need them. Trust that every small success, every step forward is something valuable to you, your future achievements, and the community that's watching.

You, the Bondsmith

In his epic fantasy novel series The Stormlight Archives, author Brandon Sanderson tells the story of a character who ascends to the magical profession of a Bondsmith. This person can connect the minds of people with a single touch. He can summon a well of light that feeds and amplifies other magical beings' powers in the vicinity. The Bondsmith does not fight; he connects. What he creates is meant to unite and elevate the people around him.

This is who I model my life after. As cheesy as it sounds, if I feel that my deeds and words build connection and opportunity between and among people, I live a full and meaningful life.

Start by being an ambitious learner. Share your journey, share your learnings, and become a person that people in your community want to engage with — because you lift up and unite everyone around you.

You, the Hero

All the historical and fictional narratives that mean the most to us involve the Hero's Journey[2]. Someone goes on an adventure, runs into trouble, things start looking better, then a catastrophe happens, the problem is overcome, and then things turn out for the better. While our personal journeys look quite different in reality, they are just as interesting to the people to whom we matter.

Jamie Russo writes about Lual, a South Sudanese man who spent his youth in a refugee camp, later teaching himself how to code, and ending up building a video game that put the player in the shoes of a refugee. The game struck a nerve, and Lual found a platform to spread his message of hope and peace. Quite literally, Lual put his uniquely personal experience into his work and created something that no one else could create the same way he did. His unique backstory gave him the power, urgency, and insight to leverage his personal journey.

In entrepreneurial terms, Lual productized himself. He took something profoundly unique and created something valuable from it. Every single one of us has some outstanding quality, experience, or disposition that we can turn into an unfair advantage: something so unique that nobody can easily copy it.

This will impact the way you engage, empower, and create valuable content. Don't create a faceless brand. Be yourself, your honest, truthful, quirky, imperfect self. Who do you think the people you care about want to follow: a fake, perfect, and idealized version that is always in full control of yourself or the version that sometimes comes up with unfunny jokes and wants to share them with your friends? Who would you rather follow if you had the choice between a plastic replica and a real human being with a story?

This also serves as a great way for people to self-select themselves out of your audience. So they don't like the things you say or the way you say them? Well, that's great news: you won't have to interact with them anymore. Why spend the energy building a relationship with people who won't reciprocate? This is not about them becoming your customers either; it really starts with making sure that you surround yourself only with people who you would want to be surrounded with in the first place.

Your Hero's Journey may not be written yet, but you can bet that people will want to be along for the ride. Be yourself, build an audience that appreciates you, and you will get your 1,000 true fans in no time.

Now let's look into how you can apply this in practice.

THE PRACTICE OF AUDIENCE-BUILDING

Audience-building is an active process, an ongoing practice that has no defined end. In this chapter, we'll examine the tools and tactics you can use to make progress along your path to domain expertise as well as building a useful product.

Hanging out on Twitter all day without a plan won't get you anywhere. Your audience-building actions need to be purposeful and intentional. Thankfully, you have the two goals to show you where you want to end up eventually. Everything you do should be in alignment with either or both goals at all times.

Many entrepreneurs are starting their first business on the side. They have a day job, a family to take care of, and any extra time is precious. Their time budget for audience-building might only be half an hour every few days or less. Let's make sure that your actions make a difference.

The first action to take when starting to build an audience is to deal with our own monkey minds. We get distracted, we lose focus, we defer work, and we ignore the hard things. Audience-building can be something we want to avoid. Maybe we're more inclined to build the product, or we want to focus on refining our vision. In short, we put this important process on the back burner.

If you want to make steady progress, I recommend setting up systems that will allow you to do so. The most important system you can set up is an Audience-Building Schedule. Throughout this chapter, I will suggest different approaches to what this schedule can look like for you. I'll also present example schedules that you can adapt to your own unique situation.

Having a schedule is halfway there. You still need to execute on it. The items in your schedule need to be done, on time, every time. For that, I recommend setting up an accountability mechanism: something that will make you want to work on your audience even when you don't feel like it.

Accountability is a tricky subject. We all experience accountability (or the lack of it) differently. If you follow Gretchen Rubin's Four Tendencies approach[1], then there are four kinds of people, all with different ways of creating accountability. Depending on how we deal with internal and external expectations, we need different methods to feel responsible for our work. Some people thrive in accountability groups like the Makerlog community or writing groups. Others feel less inclined to do a thing once someone expects them to do it. For people like this, pacts (with yourself) that threaten some small sacrifice whenever you don't fulfill your obligations work best. Many great books have been written on creating lasting habits[2] and becoming indistractable[3]. Understand how you can create accountability in your own life so that your Audience-Building Schedule can be upheld reliably.

It's imperative to set this up from the start. In the beginning, you'll be on your own. Later, you will have built an audience that communicates their expectations clearly. But when you have barely any followers, it's completely up to you to stick to your schedule.

I had to set up such a system for myself when I started writing in public. In November 2019, I started the Bootstrapped Founder blog, where I planned to write one piece of useful content every week. I knew that my tendency to find distractions in reading and learning would quickly catch up with me if I didn't set up a system. I found my accountability system in creating the Bootstrapped Founder newsletter. I posted a link to the signup page on Twitter — and this was back when I had barely any followers — and minutes later, I had a handful of hopeful and supportive people who had signed up to the newsletter.

That made all the difference. Suddenly, I wasn't writing my weekly article for myself or a nebulous "audience" anymore: here was a list of six real people who considered my work valuable. The motivation this provided me was incredibly effective: ever since, I have not missed a week of writing. In a way, I outsourced my accountability system to my audience. As long as a single person remains subscribed to my newsletter, I will write for them.

Of course, some weeks, I feel like I have nothing to say or write about. I still take the time to sift through my old blog post ideas and my Twitter interactions of the week, and quite reliably, an interesting topic will show itself eventually. Often, I have many good ideas at the same time. I park the ones I am not going to be using in a draft folder, sketching them out enough to be an outline for a later week. It's always good to have a few half-finished pieces of content lying around for when you're out of ideas.

Before we dive into the specifics of Engagement, Empowerment, and Content, let's do one last round of expectation management: *audience-building can be brutal.* It might take you a long time to get into a groove where you see results. It might feel like you're talking to a wall, and barely anyone appreciates your work. This can hurt, but I want to make it clear that this, too, shall pass. The first step is always the hardest, right?

This is particularly painful because initial traction is slow, no matter how good your content is or how often you engage with others. I have had content I wrote in my first weeks fizzle out entirely only to receive thousands of views a few months later when I reposted them to my then-larger audience. Often, people wouldn't reply to my attempts at engaging them. But after a while, after learning more about who I was and what I was about, they did. Trust the process.

Even the mightiest tree started out as a small sapling that was barely visible from afar. Over the years, your presence will become more readily noticeable, attracting more people to take a look at what you offer. It also helps to understand that audience growth isn't linear but geometric: getting from one to 100 followers will probably take the same time as getting from 100 to 1,000. This is due to network effects: the bigger your audience, the faster it will grow, since more conversations happen, more people talk to and about you, and they expose your presence to more people who might be interested. Your audience is your megaphone to build a bigger audience.

There will be days when nothing happens, no matter how much you try. And then, you'll be picked up by a large account with a gigantic audience, and you'll see levels of activities that you only ever dreamt of before. Yet, a few days later, the numbers will go down again, just a bit above where you were before. While this will feel like a wild rollercoaster ride, it's the reality of building a following: there are valleys, mountains, and all kinds of things in between. There is no certainty, only the trust in the systems you have in place to realize your audience-building efforts slowly.

Here's a practical tip for weathering those painful early days and weeks: be consistent, persistent, and insistent. Audience-building is a long-term project. You can't build an audience in a few days. This will take time and consistent effort. The regularity of your output matters more than the immediate results that you may or may not see. It will take a while for people to take notice of you. That's expected, and persistence will only set you apart from those who give up. Relationships take time to build. Consider your work in public to be an advertisement for yourself. The Advertisement Rule of 7[4] states that a customer becomes aware of a product only after being exposed to it at least seven times. Your content and interactions work the exact same way. With consistency and persistence, you will show up on more and more radars.

Finally, here's another truth: your mission is valuable. Your journey deserves to be documented. Insist on telling your story and ignore those who dismiss it. Listen to those who embrace it and build relationships with like-minded people.

Celebrate your victories, the small ones, and the big ones. It sometimes feels like the needle isn't moving much, but that's just a consequence of recency bias. The best way to combat this is by taking notes and snapshots. Not only will this keep your journey visible to you, but a screenshot of a certain follower count or a conversation with a person you never thought you'd be able to talk to are also great examples of social proof (a concept that we'll dive into later in this chapter.) Every little success is a step forward, another brick in the wall. Consider every positive interaction and every single like under your posts to be an expression of someone's belief in your mission. This Belief Capital accumulates over time, and it grows — exactly like your audience — the more you work in public.

Since we're talking numbers: don't measure follower numbers exclusively. What gets measured can become a goal in itself, and that is dangerous[5]. Inflating your follower numbers without making sure that those you actually want to interact with care about you or your work will cause more harm than it will help you. While you can't measure "the soft stuff" like the strength of connection and amount of opportunity, you can consider those factors in your decisions. Success is multivariate: a lot of independent variables contribute to the overall result. Don't just look at that one shiny number.

ENGAGEMENT

Let's talk about what exactly you can do to build an audience. Out of the three growth levers (Engagement, Empowerment, and Content), Engagement is the one that works right from the beginning. Consider this: you can always engage with someone, no matter how many followers you have. Empowering someone requires you to have an audience all ready to help you, and creating content that no one reads is a bit self-defeating. Engagement, however, is at your disposal from day one.

When you start out, you won't have much of a following, if any at all. If you post something, very few people will read it — and even fewer will share it — so that won't get you very far. However, interacting in front of an existing audience, *someone else's audience*, will allow you to encourage people to check you out, to give you a chance.

When you look at the connections between users of any social network, you will end up with a big interconnected graph of relationships. They often cluster together in little pockets, and that's where we find overlapping audiences. There is likely a big overlap in the people who follow Elon Musk and Peter Thiel. Neither will mind that their followers also follow the other account. In fact, this allows both entrepreneurs to gain new followers because their content will be exposed to a greater number of people when it gets shared.

Audience overlap is a wonderful thing in abundance-based networks. A person following Elon Musk also following you won't take anything away from Elon, but will actually make the network better: a relationship is established between all three parties, providing recommendation algorithms a better insight into what each person is interested in.

In any given community, some people already have established audiences, often of substantial size. What I recommend as the very first step to building your own audience is to do what I call the "**Audience Audition**." Put yourself in front of a reputable community member's audience and attract them to follow you as well.

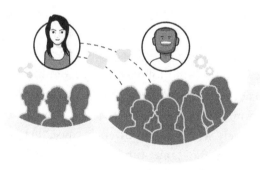

Audience Audition in a nutshell: hunt for attention, gather followers.

Audience Audition

The practice of Audience Audition has two parts: the hunting phase and the gathering phase. You hunt for opportunities to engage, and then you gather followers by actively engaging with the original author of the tweet and their followers who are responding to it.

The Hunt for Engagement Opportunities

Like in any real audition, you'll need to find the right venue to show your potential. Unlike most real-world auditions, Twitter Audience Auditions can be done completely virtually from the comfort of your home.

The first step in an Audience Audition is perhaps the most straightforward: find a Twitter account with a large audience that is likely to be interested in what you have to say. During your Embedded Exploration phase, you'll have found plenty of those influential accounts.

Depending on the size of the niche you're working with, having a "large audience" can mean anything from a few thousand to several million followers. I recommend restricting yourself to accounts with follower numbers on the lower end of this spectrum. At some point, popular Twitter users stop engaging actively with their followers because there are just too many voices. At the same time, followers of such popular accounts stop engaging with those tweets beyond liking and sharing them. Since those followers were often the supportive ones, you're left with the negative voices who take over the engagement profile: trolls, skeptics, nay-sayers. These are not the people you want to audition for.

Try finding audiences that are active and positive. They're most easily found surrounding the up-and-coming names in the field. Look for people recommending other people to follow.

The accounts mentioned there are usually somewhat popular and will continue to rise in the community. Not unlike yourself, many people will flock to them to find valuable content and connection.

Here is what to look for in a good Twitter Audience Audition candidate:

- The account posts content that triggers others to engage regularly.
- The account has a sizable following that does not overwhelm them.
- The followers are active, positive, and supportive.
- The followers consider themselves to be part of a supportive community.
- The followers are eager to invite new voices into their community.

All of this can be observed by manually sifting through an account's Twitter history, or you can use designated tools to find more information:

- Use Get The Audience to find audience-specific insights based on who engages with whom.
- Use SparkToro to find active accounts to engage with on a keyword basis.
- Use Audiense to find and filter based on influence scores.

Find a couple of accounts worth engaging with, then follow these steps:

- Take the top 5 accounts you found. You can always add more later, but you need to keep track of your first few auditions.

- Create a new Private List on Twitter (maybe name it "Audience Audition"), and add the accounts to the list.
- If you're not already using TweetDeck, start to, right now. Add a column for your private list.
- Within TweetDeck, turn on notifications for new tweets on the list, either as desktop notifications or as sounds.

Now you're ready to engage whenever they post something new.

The Rules of Successful Engagement

You're turning on notifications so you can be one of the first people to engage with a tweet. That provides a few benefits: people usually read the original tweet and one or two replies. The higher your reply is in that list, the more people will read it. More importantly, people might find value in your reply and reply to you themselves. That's what you're aiming for: inviting people to have a conversation.

Twitter usually suggests a few people who you should follow, based on your recent interactions. This happens in your Twitter client, and it happens in the Twitter client of the people you are "auditioning" for. That's where you want to show up. You want the Twitter algorithm to recommend you as the perfect person for them to follow. Getting someone to interact with you and then fondly remember that interaction when Twitter suggests following you is your goal for every interaction.

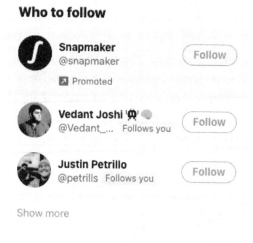

Looks like Vedant and Justin were successful at getting my attention.

Being one of the top replies to any tweet will also have an interesting psychological effect called the Gestalt law of proximity[1]. Due to humans being very visual beings, we consider physical proximity to be an indicator of categorical similarity. If one thing is close to another thing, then they are perceived to be related. Now consider how this works on Twitter: the closer your Twitter avatar is to the picture of your engagement target, the more people will believe you and that account to be similar — and then follow you.

Make Yourself Presentable: Avatar, Bio, Pinned Tweet

Now that we're talking about Twitter avatars, let's focus on making yourself presentable. Back during your Embedded Exploration, you already made sure you were trustworthy and respectable. Let's revisit this now that you're actively looking for followers.

Your profile page should be an invitation: an invitation to

become a friend. I mean it! Humans make up their minds about another person within a fraction of a second. The more you appear to be someone they'd want to hang out with on their couch or in their backyard, the more likely you are to start a relationship from your profile page alone. Now, this doesn't mean you should put up a picture of yourself flipping burgers. Just consider the feelings you want to evoke in the subconscious of a person who comes to your profile: positivity, enthusiasm, and joy.

Choose your avatar picture carefully. It will be your visual brand. Find an image that you can use for a long time: people quickly get confused when the only visual thing about an account suddenly changes. They won't recognize your face anymore and will stop engaging with your content. While they will get used to your new avatar picture over time, you can avoid this dip.

The same goes for your Twitter handle: pick one, and stay with it. You have a few choices here:

- **Use your full name**, like "Arvid Kahl." That's my preference, as this shows professionalism as well as owning your identity. It makes building a personal brand very easy, as your full name will be attached to every conversation you're in.
- **Use a pseudonym**, which I don't recommend. While it's acceptable in many communities, people will be hesitant to trust accounts that act secretively about their identity. In a trust-based economy, making it harder for people to see that you're trustworthy is not a good idea. I personally use pseudonyms whenever I *don't* want to build an audience, like in online games.
- Use an "**action name**," like "Arvid is writing a book," to indicate what you're currently doing. This works best for established personal brands who want to

keep surprising their followers. If you're into that, do that once you have an audience, but avoid it when you're starting.

- **Use a "business name,"** like "Arvid (PermanentLink)" to make people aware of your business. While this can work, it will make it hard for people to differentiate you as a person from your product. It will taint your personal account, particularly when you are not talking about business. Consider the impact that a screenshot of a tweet about a particularly controversial political or social issue might have on your product brand.

Where your picture is supposed to be visually inviting, your bio should arouse your potential follower's curiosity. There are several ways to do that, so find a unique combination of these approaches that works for you:

- **Share what you talk about.** Writing expert Julian Shapiro's bio starts with this impactful statement: "Tweeting about writing and clear thinking." It couldn't be any more explicit about what topics you can expect this person to tweet.
- **Share things you are.** Dan Kuschell lists these facts about him in his bio: "Father, Husband, Entrepreneur, Author, Speaker and Mentor." This invites potential followers to imagine him as a multi-faceted human being worth interacting with.
- **Share what you are working on.** Jack Butcher's bio is concise and tells you which projects he runs: "Experimenting, sharing results: @visualizevalue, @value." No fluff, just to-the-point information.
- **Make jokes.** When you start reading Craig Burgess's bio, you encounter this: "I'm the best

designer that my mum knows. 62% designer / 37% marketer / 3% mathematician." Who wouldn't want to have a chat with someone who is humble, funny, and clearly a bit provocative. However, use humor carefully. Your personality needs to match the style of your bio.

You can tell that there is no surefire way to write a great bio. When in doubt, check out how your Audience Audition target Twitter accounts have their bio set up. There likely is a common theme among them, and even if there isn't, you'll be fairly safe imitating the structure and style of a popular account's bio.

Let's talk about links on your Twitter profile. When people check you out, you are actually in a conundrum: will they immediately follow you? Then you wouldn't need a link on your profile at all. Will they want to check out your link? That would make them go off Twitter, and you can only hope they come back to follow you. Phew, that's a tough choice.

Generally, I recommend having a link on your Twitter profile. Give people an option to learn more about you. Linking to your personal website or most important project is a good idea. Not every visitor to your profile will click that link, but the content you provide on your personal blog or website might just convince a person to follow you. If you don't have a personal page, consider setting up a little static link page on linktree or bio.fm and fill it with interesting links to your projects and content on the web.

Finally, let's talk about an important part of your Twitter real estate that many entrepreneurs ignore: your pinned tweet. This is the first tweet that people will see on your profile, and it's "above the fold": it's right there for everyone to see.

Your pinned tweet should be your best tweet. That can mean many things. It might be your best-performing tweet to show how much engagement you can create or the best-received one as a sign of social proof. You could show your best work or your latest project. Personally, I always keep my most recent project announcement tweet pinned. It shows not only what I created, but usually also where people can purchase it. The massive amount of likes and replies further encourage people to check out my work.

Don't let your pinned tweet go stale. A tweet from last month is fine, and if it's really good, a few months of age might show how well it ripened. However, if your best tweet hasn't been surpassed for the last three years, people will start wondering why. It's like using your college yearbook photo (or, even more embarrassingly, your college yearbook quote) to show people who you are. We all grow, and we expect people to show off their most recent accomplishments.

A Word About Manners

Your Audience Audition is a public act. There will be a record of it for a long time. People will be able to find your public interactions unless you willfully delete them. There are archives to retrieve these things if you do, and this will cast an even more shady light on you.

Always act with the understanding that you are portraying your sincere self in a community that expects people to be honest about themselves. If you lie or start manipulating people and relationships for a short-term gain, your long-term plans won't come to fruition.

So, here are things to avoid:

- **Don't be needy.** Asking for people to follow you is not how you make friends. People will consider you to be someone who accumulates Twitter followers purely for the sake of numbers. People love to follow others because they think it provides them with something. If you ask for a follow, you're making it about yourself instead.

- **Don't spam.** It's great to be the first reply to a popular account's tweet. Don't try to be the first reply on *all* of their tweets. People like that are called "reply guys," and they are shunned for gaming the system. An Audience Audition is not a competition to see who can show up the fastest every single time. It's about providing meaningful contributions to an ongoing conversation.

- **Don't condescend.** This is an Audience Audition, not Thanksgiving Dinner with your weird cousins. People are watching you closely, and you are trying to attract kind and interested people. The best way to do that is to be kind and interesting yourself. Keep back the retorts, the "but actually's," even when you usually would launch into a tirade. Instead, either don't engage at all or provide a helpful alternative perspective without judgment.

In a minute, we'll talk about how you can craft a message that will resonate with people. Before we can write an engaging message, we need to understand the context in which it will appear: the conversation.

Conversations are at the Core of Engagement

Yelling into the void won't get you anywhere. This is particularly clear while you have zero followers, but it remains true even when you have an audience. Talking about something that people don't expect or want to talk about is just like speaking to them in a language they don't understand: it's a waste of their time as much as yours.

The easiest way to understand a community is to consider it

to be one extensive narrative, an epic story, that consists of many smaller conversations. If you look at the Indie Hacker community, the narrative arc is the hero's journey from nothing to financial security by building their own digitally enabled business. Within that ever-repeating story, different themes appear every now and then, just like in a classical symphony. They harmonize with each other, they rhyme, but they are distinct and different from each other.

The moment you chime in, the moment you contribute to these narratives and themes, you become interesting. People will recognize your shared interests, and they will consider you as one of their own. Therefore, the goal of audience-building is to find your place in the grand orchestra that is your community by engaging with useful and thought-provoking content that your fellow community members expect and value. You will find this place by participating in all the conversations of your niche.

By doing this regularly, you will attract high-value followers. That's great for you, but it has an additional favorable side-effect: it's also community-building! You're providing another node in the network, another perspective on content that was created by others. Community organizers recognize people who do this consciously and deliberately and reward them with benevolence and exposure. We'll dive into this further in the Empowerment section, but as a helpful guide, consider maximizing the community's positive impact in every interaction you have.

People look for many things in a conversation. Here are the main themes that I have run into and how I usually engage with them:

- **People look for help.** This can be a specific problem or a more general question, and it's usually phrased as a direct complaint or a question. If I have something immediately helpful to say, I reply right there and then. If I can't help but know someone who could, I try to get them involved in the conversation. When I don't know anyone, in particular, I usually retweet the plea for help, hoping that someone among my followers can help out.

- **People look for moral support.** Usually, in the wake of a tough challenge or some sort of failure, people will seek a conversation. The best thing to do here is to show empathy and validate this person's feelings and experiences. I am often tempted to help with actionable advice here, but this might actually be counterproductive. I've learned to listen for a while to determine if help is appreciated or if the original poster is just looking for a sympathetic ear.

- **People look for distraction.** They bring up conversation topics that are controversial or polarizing to avoid working on the things that actually matter. While I tend to avoid these conversations, they might spark interesting sub-conversations with people who are interested in a meaningful exchange about the subject. I engage when I see those people interacting and ignore the discussion otherwise.

- **People ask for alternative viewpoints.** While this is a rare conversation, it might be one of the most instructive. Whenever people share their position on an issue and ask for another perspective, I enjoy engaging with them. The important part is never to dismiss their perspective when presenting yours. These conversations make prime targets for sourcing interesting content ideas for yourself. After all, you'll always find opposing concepts and ideas and the contentious battle between them. These points of friction are often central to the overarching narrative of the community: "Should founders bootstrap or take funding?" – "Tabs or spaces?" – "Is Solopreneurship better than having Co-Founders?"

Clearly, those questions have no objectively correct answer. The debates around these topics are instructive as they enable people to share their anecdotes and find common themes and interesting learnings.

- **People want to refine their vague idea into something concrete.** No matter if it's a knitting project or a newly envisioned business idea, people seek help in their community when it comes to testing and validating ideas. I love those opportunities. It gives me the chance to think deeply about an idea, add my personal experience to it, and then present my conclusions not only to the person who asked but also to the community that's watching. Insightful and creative replies to questions like this will help you quickly acquire a reputation as a thoughtful subject matter expert.
- **People want to share their journey.** Whether it's reaching a certain amount of Monthly Recurring Revenue or a particularly nasty Customer Cancellation Email, I love to engage with a fellow entrepreneur when something meaningful happens in their lives. Bolstering another entrepreneur's confidence is fun and generates good community vibes, establishing you as a team player.

These are the most common engagement targets that I regularly work with. To give you a well-rounded perspective, here are the things I try not to engage with:

- **Fishing for compliments.** There is a thin line between building in public and trying to get attention for attention's sake. I only want to engage with people who build in public for the community's sake as much as their own. Selfishly occupying other people's time without giving back something useful is not something I will encourage or endorse. If you engage with these people too much, other community members will see you as an opportunist, just like the person you engaged with.
- **Looking for pity without a way out.** I will engage with people who need moral support. I will ignore those who want a shoulder to cry on without also considering ways to get back on track.
- **Clear examples of unreflected cognitive biases.** Particularly if a person gets defensive when people helpfully point out highly flawed arguments, I hold back for a few minutes. If the conversation derails into an argument instead of a healthy debate, I will not engage.
- **Baiting and trolling.** Clearly, these conversations don't contribute to furthering the goals of your community. I often get mad about something, and I am very tempted to respond, but in the end, I try to step back and look at how much good this would do, and it's usually not much. Find something better to spend your attention on.

So, with the context being clear, let's look into crafting an engaging message.

What a Good Audience Audition Tweet Looks Like

Any tweet you send out for your Audience Audition should do one or more of these four things: Expand, Focus, Syndicate, or Invite.

These four options are essentially zooming in and zooming out along two axes: the level of detail and the exposure of the conversation. You can either a) focus on the details and get particular people to join or b) you can expand the scope of the topic and expose it to a larger audience.

Expand

Zoom out of a specific issue and bring in some broader insight, transferring information from another field or perspective into the conversation. This is most easily done with a perspective shift:

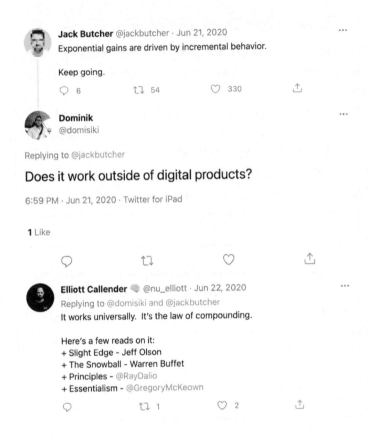

In this tweet, Jack, an experienced player in the digital content realm, talks about iteration. Dominik asks about expanding this conversation's scope, and Elliot obliges, both introducing an interesting concept and even referencing a few sources.

Focus

Zoom into an issue even more. Get into the nitty-gritty, find the underlying motivations and concepts, and shine a light on hidden details. Follow-up questions allow for this to happen.

Specifically, they have a high chance of triggering a direct inter-action with the original author, leading to more exposure to their audience as someone worth answering to, like in this example:

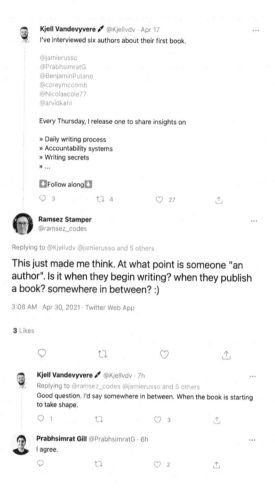

Kjell replies to Ramsez's request for elaboration on defini-tion of what makes authors call themselves an author. This engagement even triggers other audience members to join in.

Syndicate

Expose the conversation to a bigger audience. This increases the amount of learning that anyone interested in the subject might experience. You can do this by either retweeting or, better yet, quote-tweeting the original tweet.

Why quote-tweet? You get to take your own spin on the topic while still enjoying the engagement of the original tweet. Additionally, Twitter will show you your own engagement metrics on a quotes tweet, while they don't do that for simple retweets. While this isn't too important, it's nice to see how many people saw your quote tweet and chose to engage with it.

Exposing someone else's content to your own growing audience won't go unnoticed, particularly when it results in someone else jumping in and helping out. Whenever you don't have anything meaningful to contribute but still want to be supportive, start sharing.

Invite

Expose specific experts to this conversation. Bringing in the expertise needed to solve a problem will increase the quality of a conversation significantly. This is targeted syndication: you make sure that a particular person gets to see this conversation. I do this whenever I know that the only thing standing between a problem and its solution is for a particular expert to chime in.

Inviting people to a particular conversation creates a connection in a few ways:

- The original author benefits from learning about another expert in the field.
- Your Audition Audience learns that you are a person who enjoys building relationships.

- The expert you bring in recognizes you as someone who considers them reputable.
- You get to enjoy the resulting conversation.

That's all there is to writing an effective engagement tweet: Expand, Focus, Syndicate, Invite. As long as you do at least one of these things, your engagement will add value to the conversation, and your Audition Audience will notice.

Always be appreciative. No matter if you agree, add further information, or present a different opinion, you are acting under public scrutiny. Make it clear that you're operating from a compassionate place.

In any case, the main point is to respond to the original message with some form of value. It doesn't have to be the world's smartest answer, but it has to contribute to the overall solution of a problem.

Good Questions are Intentional and Contextual

Asking a question is a great way to show interest. But just asking for the sake of asking is not enough.

Let's say you want to engage with someone who just posted this message: *"Software Engineers just don't like paying money for solutions to their problems."*

"Why is that?" is a boring question. It's 100% demanding, without offering any substantial value. Even though it expresses curiosity, this kind of question often won't get you a response. It's short, it looks careless, and it feels almost disrespectful.

A good question provides intent and context. How about: *"I have experienced similar problems in my job running a SaaS for Frontend Developers. Now that I work with DevOps Engineers, I don't see as much of that anymore. Why do you think that could be?"*

This question invites a perspective shift and a reasoned response. It focuses on a particular part of the mentioned audience, and it comes with anecdotal context for the original author to consider in their reply. This will also be an interesting opportunity for other community members to chime in with their own anecdotes, adding value to the whole conversation.

Things to Avoid during an Audience Audition

To make sure you don't only see the happy path, let me share a few examples of how you should not engage, and why.

Dismissing, bad-mouthing, and trash talking. The moment you think you're better than someone else, more knowledgeable, and you want to show them, you're acting from a zero-sum perspective. Instead of elevating another person, calling them out in public creates a negative space. Negative thoughts will attract other negative thinkers to that space and then to you. Ask yourself: do you want *these* people to follow you wherever you go?

Now, there is a difference between disagreement and putting someone down. That difference is conversational respect. Since that can't always be implied, state it outright. A *"Thank you for that perspective, I was not aware of that. Here is what I am thinking..."* will be received as a civil disagreement, while "You're wrong about this and here is why..." is a blatant attack — no matter how much you believe yourself to be in the right.

(Wrongly) applied fallacies. Whenever you feel you should point out a shortcoming in someone's argument, make sure you step back and see if your own response is not falling prey to a fallacy[2]. You won't make a good impression on your audition audience if you use ad hominem attacks or fall into the No-True-Scotsman fallacy while debating with another expert in your field. Rhetoric has no place in your Audience Audition.

Begging for engagement, likes, or followers. Never *ever* beg for people to follow you. Not only is it desperate, but it also communicates a few things to your Audition Audience:

- You're not able to create valuable content that would attract them naturally.
- You're looking for statistics over real relationships.
- You want them to do something without giving them anything in return.
- You're not interested in earning their trust and affection.
- You care more about yourself than you care about your audience.

I've said this many times: all your actions are public. Just like you wouldn't want to get your spot in the orchestra because you begged during the audition, don't ask people to follow you during your Audience Audition. A following that you earned through doing the work is so much more rewarding than a few pity follows and being dismissed by the people who matter.

Now, that sums up the Audience Audition process. I prefer having a structured approach for my social media engagement. The alternative is hoping to find a diamond in the rough by randomly crossing their path. It's much more effective to look for interesting followers where they are already engaging in conversations. This approach relies much less on serendipity than on setting up the right systems.

This is also an ongoing process. No matter if you have one follower, 500 or 20,000, you'll want to audition for other accounts' audiences consistently. I am doing this still, every day, and I don't intend to stop. My audience is growing, our industry is growing, and I know that I will grow with them by putting myself out there.

EMPOWERMENT

Growth is something that can be made visible. The act of empowerment will help you do that for yourself and, more interestingly, for others.

Building in public is a team sport. While you're the one doing the "building," the "public" will be there to follow your journey. They will see your personal growth from your regular updates on what challenges, successes, and failures you encounter along your path. They will comment on your posts, support you when you're down, and advise you when you need guidance.

One way to give back is to reciprocate. Were people appreciative of your comments on their tweets? Did they engage with you, taking those conversations to new levels of insight? Now is your turn to help them.

The easiest way to empower someone is to make them feel seen and recognized. Thankfully, nothing is easier than that on social media platforms such as Twitter. Here are a few surefire ways that will help someone, without costing you anything:

- You can amplify their message by sharing it with a larger or different audience.
- You can amplify their message by endorsing it.
- You can boost their confidence by congratulating them for a success.
- You can boost their confidence by consoling them when they suffer through failure.
- You can cement their reputation by inviting them to help someone else as an expert.
- You can cement their reputation by calling out the positive impact their actions had on you and your peers.

None of these activities will cost you more than a few seconds of your time and a few clicks. They can mean a whole lot to the person you're empowering, though. No matter if someone already has an audience or not, they will always be happy to reach more people and grow their personal and professional brands.

Always consider the abundance mindset. If you can make someone feel better, that's a net gain because it won't make anyone else feel worse. In an expansive community, lifting up others is how the community grows.

Consider this chain of events:

- Someone with a very small following has a problem with their business.
- They ask a question on Twitter, like, *"Hey, does anyone know anything about pricing your SaaS plans? I don't know where to start."*
- You're not a SaaS expert, but you know that a few people in your audience have built successful businesses before. You retweet their question.

- Within minutes, three of your followers respond to
  the original question and provide helpful answers.

All you did was click twice to retweet their question. But the result of this interaction is spectacularly rich:

- You enabled experts to voice their opinions. They will
  now consider you a facilitator of their reputation.
- You allowed a person in need to find an answer to
  their question. They will now consider you an enabler
  of their entrepreneurial success.
- You showed your audience that you altruistically care
  about others' problems, and you established a
  connection between people who likely didn't know
  each other before. They will now consider you a
  promoter of community relationship-building.

From one single selfless retweet, you just gained a reputation in three different areas. Empowerment is maybe the most powerful tool at your disposal.

Let's talk about a few other benefits around empowering and lifting up other people.

Making Friends Has a Place in Business

The moment you stop considering Twitter a "content distribution channel" and start seeing it as a way to build a "community of peers," things will start changing. By acting in the interest of the community, you begin attracting community-minded people. The more you empower other people in the community, the more they will empower you.

This sounds like a selfless act at first, but it's really not. Be selfish in a way that benefits other people. That's a win-win situation for everyone involved, and it will create long-lasting benefits.

For this to happen reliably, you will start building meaningful relationships. You're making friends, not just followers. After all, people stay friends for a long time precisely because their relationship is mutually enjoyable and beneficial. An honest and authentic relationship is so much more interesting than having a shallow and superficial connection with a person. This is best made visible in the concept of the "Opportunity Surface."

Building an Opportunity Surface

It is unavoidable that luck plays a part in your entrepreneurial success. Here are a few stories the likes of which you'll hear over and over:

- "I had a chance encounter with another founder from my home town at a conference, and they introduced me to my fellow co-founder a month later at a dinner."
- "I struck up a conversation with a random prospective customer on Twitter, and two years later, they told their friend who worked at an enterprise business about my product. All of a sudden, this giant corporation became my biggest customer."
- "I researched my audience on Facebook, and an ad for a software product popped up by chance. I checked it out, it wasn't very good, and within a year, I had built a much more helpful competitor."

None of these things happened on purpose; they happened through sheer serendipity — or did they?

Throughout many stories of "how lucky things just

happened" to people, the common thread is that they all set themselves up to be lucky[1]. If you want to see a meteor shower, you have to look at the sky and wait for it to happen. If you're not looking, you won't ever see the majestic rocks burning up in our atmosphere. If you're not preparing the right way, you won't accomplish what you want to do.

All "tales of luck" start with an action, a preparation of sorts. Look at the above examples. If those people hadn't gone to that conference or sent that Twitter message, the events that led to their success would not have happened. Of course, they didn't know that these particular consequences would occur, but they knew that they *might*.

Lucky opportunities are serendipitous in the sense that they are hard to predict and happen at random points in time and space. Usually, they don't even look that interesting. But in retrospect, after one thing leads to another, they are the key events that allowed for the result to unfold. The people who have understood that these events are occurring so randomly often focus on allowing for as many as possible to happen for them. They treat every action they take as a candidate for serendipity.

Most of all, people who have good things happen to them understand that "luck" is little more than highly delayed gratification. By doing the work that may not benefit you immediately but has a potentially large upside in the future, you will unlock those serendipitous possibilities. Suppose you only ever do "business as usual," chase for that one next follower or try to sell to that one next customer. In that case, you won't ever notice those little moments of human connection that unlock the luckiest of consequences.

That's what the Opportunity Surface concept is about: taking time to invite in serendipity by doing as much as possible to connect with other people meaningfully.

Allowing for Reciprocation

Let's get a bit more pragmatic here. Your "luck anticipation battery" can be charged by empowering others. Whenever you help someone selflessly, other people will take notice. It will just be a little bit, a tiny amount of trust, but over time — while you consistently and persistently empower others — they will understand you to be deserving of the opportunity.

I finally understood this when I wrote my first book, *Zero to Sold*. In the months leading up to the book's release, I made a point of being extremely active in the community, both on Twitter and in the public forums that my readers often visit. I would share my work, my progress and help other founders with my insights. Where I didn't have anything to add, I would amplify their messages, hoping they'd find help that way. Meanwhile, I shared interesting links and celebrated other founders' successes in my newsletter.

The day I released my book, something spectacular happened. I had a Twitter following of just over 4,000 then, which I had slowly built for the past eight months. My followers immediately retweeted and liked my launch tweet and started commenting on it with good wishes and encouragement. Then, just minutes later, the first screenshot of Amazon purchase pages showed up. Just after that, people posted actual pictures of themselves holding Kindles with my book loaded up. Within 24 hours, I had sold over 350 copies — as a first-time author without any prior success.

I later realized that this was an outlet: a way for people to give back to me after I had given them something for free for such a long time. I had slowly increased my opportunity surface over time, building up small bits of reputation and goodwill with many founders in the space. And now it was their turn to show me their appreciation.

Over the next few days and weeks, people continued to

tweet pictures of their purchases and did my marketing for me. Now that the paperback version was starting to arrive in people's homes, they even took selfies with my book. Even better: they took pictures with their pets sitting on my book. I was blown away by such a sweet and encouraging response.

None of this had to happen. I didn't ask people to do this for me. My followers and readers did this because they found me worthy of their support, both because I had provided a lot of valuable content and because I was such an active part of their community. None of the actions I took were aimed at making people buy the book. Of course, I always hoped that someone would take a look at my work, but I never envisioned this intensity.

People were waiting to reciprocate. The time invested in engagement and empowerment in the months before the launch created this tension that was released on my launch day.

The Spirit of Entrepreneurship: Kindness and Altruism

Selflessness and entrepreneurship feel contradictory. But that's just a mirage of the hypercapitalist doctrine that resulted in predatorial practices and winner-take-all markets. Luckily, you have the choice to act differently in the Indie Hacker and Boot-strapped Founder space. The presence of the abundance mindset allows for behavior that is not exclusively selfish.

In fact, there are quite a few founders who only got to build their indie businesses because of others' kindness.

In a conversation on how much "perceived luck" has influenced his entrepreneurial life, Pierre de Wulf shared his story about how his employer supporting him on his way to getting ScrapingBee off the ground. In an act of unanticipated kindness, his employer set things up so that Pierre had full benefits for a year after leaving his position. That was very fortunate since his SaaS made no money for its first year.

Without this act of decency and support, Pierre might have needed to find another job and wouldn't be running a sustainable SaaS business, which he co-founded with his life-long friend, Kevin. You can sense Pierre's gratitude for this in his every action: Pierre is outspoken about his journey, he's building in public, and he is supporting his fellow indie hackers on a daily basis.

The best-performing marketing action we took for FeedbackPanda when we were growing our customer base and audience for our Online Teacher SaaS was to make our newsletters about our existing customers. Every week, we'd highlight one particular customer after they sent us a photo of themselves and gave us some insights into their backstory as English teachers. Our customers loved this and assigned us the brand of being an empathetic and selfless company. For our users, we were part of their community, not just another business trying to take their money.

The Act of Entrepreneurship: Solving Problems and Cultivating Community

Don't get me wrong, making money is still at the core of running a business. Without a solution to a critical problem for customers who have a budget, you're not running a business. That's a charity project at best. People pay for solutions to their problems. But that doesn't necessarily need to be a classical product.

Building a solution is one thing, but building a community for people to solve their problems themselves is another. Andrew Hodson, an auto-mechanic turned self-taught tech entrepreneur, turned his insight into the pet and livestock hauling industry into a marketplace called Hauling Buddies. Before he went and built the product, he did something equally impressive: he started with a few Facebook groups. Created by a family member who did a lot of horse hauling over the weekends, one particular group connected and matched horse owners and animal haulers group.

Here is where Andrew initially learned the ropes of administrating a problem-driven community. Since that Facebook group grew to five figures in size, he could leverage his experience and joined similar groups, where he quickly became either the group owner or an administrator. Over time, Andrew took over the reins of half a dozen such groups and learned everything he needed to know about the real problems felt by those very real people — and animals. Eventually, the Facebook-based mixing and matching motivated him to build a dedicated marketplace, and Hauling Buddies was born.

Andrew still uses these groups as lead funnels into his marketplace product. In fact, he found that hauling businesses made for wonderful group administrators due to their industry knowledge and business sense. He essentially turned a bunch of Facebook groups into a self-moderating business empire that drives quality leads to haulers who are involved in their community. Talk about empowerment.

Amplification is Encouragement

One of the reasons why sharing other people's stories and connecting them is so powerful is that you will strengthen their resolve every time you amplify their messages. Every time you connect an eager person with a bigger audience, their cause is validated, and they will feel encouraged to continue on their journey.

Confidence is one of the biggest gifts you can give to your community. Many people struggle, and it takes them a lot of courage to reach out to their community. You'll be lifting them up by amplifying their content, and it won't cost you anything at all.

There is a dark side to a community where everybody is constantly encouraging each other in their beliefs: it creates echo chambers. Now, this doesn't always have to create impenetrable filter bubbles that completely isolate community members from alternative viewpoints. Still, there is always a chance that potentially useful ideas and concepts might be ignored just because they are new.

So what can you do? I recommend doing the exact same things you'd do in your business: create an atmosphere of positivity while transferring knowledge and insights across communities. Particularly when you have experience in multiple industries, you can leverage that knowledge to infuse the ongoing discussion with anecdotes and learnings that bring in alternative viewpoints to challenge vicious circle arguments.

Blind encouragement is also not very fruitful. If you see founders struggling because they are doing something that — at least to me — seems obviously wrong and destructive, I usually reach out to them in a private message before I engage with their content. I try to understand more about their situation so that I can give public advice that is productive, respectful, and will be both an encouragement for the person who wrote the original message and for people who are in similar situations.

Empowerment comes in many shapes. I want to end this chapter with a few ideas that will help you find your own unique way of encouraging and supporting other community members:

- Share insightful tweets by influential thinkers in your space.
- Share articles that you have found on the web that your followers can learn from.
- Help someone find beta testers for their prototypes.
- Connect someone with an expert that can solve their question.

- Show someone an example of what they are looking for.
- Celebrate someone's success with them.
- Encourage someone who failed at something.
- Expose someone to a different perspective or approach that they're not yet aware of.
- Inspire someone to take the plunge/to go ahead with something that they are dreading.
- Reassure someone that the community has got their back and will support them.
- Include someone in the conversation who should be part of it.
- Give someone more reach because they are just starting out but have important contributions.
- Expose someone who hasn't yet found their community to your audience.
- Help people deal with emotional stress by providing an outlet and showing how shared their pain is.
- Validate someone's work by encouraging them to make more of it.

This list could go on forever — and it should for you. Whatever you can think of that might lift up other people, do it regularly. Be the community member you want the others to be.

VALUABLE CONTENT

Now that we've looked into Engagement and Empowerment, let's dive into the third pillar of audience growth. Producing valuable content is the most reliable way to become a reputable professional. After all, if you have helpful things to say that positively impact the lives of those who listen to you, that makes you the domain expert you set out to be. Let's find out what steps you can take to get there. We'll start by dissecting the term "valuable content."

What's Content?

The most important thing to understand about content is that it can take many shapes. I used to think that creating content meant "writing an article," but that's a very narrow definition. In fact, it is a limiting definition because it severely restricts your imagination.

A quote can be content. Asking the right question at the right time can inspire people to reconsider long-held beliefs: definitely content. In fact, the mere act of asking is content, regardless of the question itself. Having a conversation with an expert on a subject you know very much or very little about is a spectacle in the best sense of the word: people love to see it, as they can learn something about themselves, you, the expert, and the subject matter in the process. Sharing an article you wrote: clearly a piece of content-creation as well as an act of con, just like asking a question. But so is showing a screenshot of how many people that article attracted to your blog.

The best and most encompassing definition of "content" that I could find is "information made available" — and I believe that is a pretty insightful definition. Not only do you need information, but you need to make it available for someone to consume. And that brings us to the other part of "valuable content."

What is Value?

For most of us, things that we consider valuable are things that are useful to us, in one way or another. Having something of value means receiving some sort of benefit. That can be monetary gain, peace of mind, enjoyment, stimulation, serenity, connection, and much more. In essence, value is a form of gain.

For content to be valuable to your audience, someone other than yourself needs to gain something from it. If you can teach someone something or make them feel better about themselves with something that you posted on Twitter, congratulations are in order: you have just created valuable content.

This is all there is to content. It doesn't have to be half a book of text. A well-timed emoji, a funny meme, or an encouraging "You got this!" is all you need. Of course, since value is something measurable, some content will be more valuable than the other. That doesn't mean you should skip the small stuff: you're not a content machine, and you'd better stay away from appearing to be one.

Avoiding Content Overflow

Beware of becoming a content spammer. The ideas introduced in this chapter will give you many ideas, and you might want to try all of them at once. Pace yourself. Consider what releasing a new piece of content 12 times a day will do to your followers' activity streams. While they follow you for your insights, they also follow other people for the same reasons. They surely wouldn't want you to spam their timeline.

The best way to figure out how much content you should be posting is to figure out how much a few notable people in your community are tweeting on any given day and take the average. Try to aim for that number, maybe a bit less. The idea is to stay within the amount of content people have come to expect in their community. Be a team player, and don't hog the activity stream. Tools like SocialBlade will help you find these numbers.

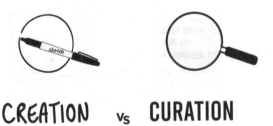

CREATION vs CURATION

Creation vs Curation

Your audience isn't the only one at risk of being overwhelmed. Creating content might seem like an impossible endeavor, particularly when you're just starting out. Everyone else is so skilled at writing engaging tweets and articles, how are you supposed to compete with such experienced creators? They write these things as if it was nothing, but you've been sitting there editing a single engagement tweet for 12 minutes and you're still unhappy with it.

Fear not! There is a path towards becoming an experienced creator, and it does not exclusively involve creating bad things until you create good things. While this will need to happen, too, you can learn the ropes of creation by starting with a focus on *curation*.

Finding interesting things that others have created and presenting them to an interested audience is all around us. Museums, Spotify playlists, art exhibits, libraries, even Twitter itself: all of these places and services show you things that other people have done, and that you might like.

I mentioned this earlier: content that no one gets to see can't be valuable. Creation without curation is a hollow act. Consider that whenever you share someone else's work, in a list of resources or as a recommendation, you're serving both them and your audience by connecting thoughts, ideas, concepts, and people who might not have found each other if it wasn't for your curative efforts.

Creation is a handful of polished and cut gemstones, and curation brings them together in a finely crafted setting — and jewelry emerges. The world needs both content and curation, and it will be easier to get started on your path to creating beautiful content by curating it. If you want to be like the best, you have to have seen their work. Curation will allow for that.

The remainder of this book will introduce all kinds of

content. Each of them can be a creative or a curative effort. Both are fine, and they will all resonate with your audience. You decide.

Many Kinds of Content

I have found that different communities prefer and reward many kinds of content quite differently. What matters most is that whatever you do, you contribute to the community in some way. Even when you are advertising your products — and we'll get to that particular kind of content later — make sure they allow your fellow community members to benefit from your message.

That said, here are a few interesting content ideas for your audience-building efforts. Whenever you need some inspiration, consult this list and see how you can either create or curate something valuable for your audience.

The Insight

Creating the most basic piece of content involves you writing about something you know. That content should be insightful, actionable, and understandable. Here's a great example by *Atomic Habits* author James Clear:

James Clear ✓
@JamesClear

Fear of failure is higher when you're not working on the problem.

If you are taking action, you are less worried about failure because you realize you can influence the outcome.

4:49 PM · Jan 27, 2021 · Twitter Web App

1,673 Retweets   **91** Quote Tweets   **7,329** Likes

Quite the insight, isn't it? Experts talking about the things they understand best is one of the main reasons why people follow them. Most of the time, insightful content is dense and quotable. Some Twitter accounts, unsurprisingly those of writers, are particularly good at coming up with short messages that pack a lot of wisdom in just a few characters.

Here's another one, by writing educator David Perell:

David Perell @david_perell · Jan 28
Write with the heart, edit with the mind.

Nobody sees your first draft, so pour your soul onto the page. Be bold and controversial. Let the wisdom of logic wait until the editing phase.

Writer's block happens when you're too judgemental with yourself when you start writing.

♡ 9   ⟲ 43   ♡ 346   ⬆

It will take you a good while to come up with really well-phrased insights. That's why you should start by just sharing what you know and trust that, over time, you'll refine your writing skills. What matters is that you share, not that it's perfectly phrased.

Here are a few things to consider when crafting insightful tweets:

- **Make them quotable.** The shorter the message, the better.
- **Be distinctive.** Add your own voice to the tweet. When in doubt, ask yourself: "Would a faceless corporation tweet this?" If so, add more personality.
- **Talk to people, not at them.** It's often a thin line, but nobody wants to hear a lecture. Be conversational in your tone.
- **Avoid commonplaces.** If the thing you're about to say has been said 40 times today already, you might want to find something more exciting. At the same time, consider that not everyone is at the same place on their learning journey. Something that might sound obvious to you might be meaningful information to them. Strike a balance, which is best done by observing how influential thinkers in the niche approach this.
- **Use imaged instead of words.** If you need more text than 280 characters (but don't want to use multiple tweets). A well-designed image also allows you to design the layout of your message. Just be sure to take accessibility[1] into consideration.
- **Cool it on the hashtags.** One or two are more than enough. I personally only use them when they relate to a time-sensitive matter like a social movement or an in-group event like #BuildInPublic.
- **Use clear, familiar, and attractive language.** Teach yourself to write good copy using positive power words[2] and the jargon of your niche audience.

- **Use well-designed images.** People expect high-quality images that are relevant to their interests.

It should go without saying that replying to someone who engages with your tweet is extremely powerful. With such a reply, you validate and grow your relationship with the person who responded. At the same time, your content sees more engagement, making it visible to a larger audience. If you don't know what to say, just thank them for their response. That's all it takes.

The Thread

Just as much as some people love short, insightful messages, others really appreciate very long, insightful messages. Some Twitter accounts are known for lengthy Twitter threads, while others restrict themselves to short single-tweet insights. And, of course, you can mix and match.

There are two approaches to the tweet thread. Either you write a longer piece of text and split it into individual tweets, or you curate a list of interesting resources in the shape of a thread.

Let's look at a creation-centric Twitter thread (or at least a part of it):

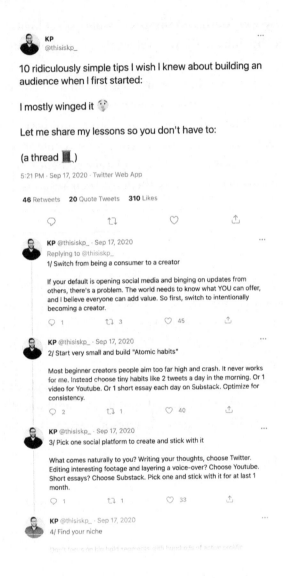

KP, a strong proponent of the Build in Public movement, shares 10 insightful thoughts in one message. It's a collection of connected pieces of advice. The Twitter thread is the perfect way of sharing all these messages in one cohesive unit. The first tweet is particularly well-crafted: KP promises 10 insights, tells you something surprising about them, and tells you the value of reading further along his thread.

While individual tweets might get a lot of engagement, insightful threads are supercharged engagement magnets. Here are a few tips that will help you create well-performing threads:

- **The first tweet is an anchor.** If you can get people to engage with this tweet, they will pull the other tweets along. Your first tweet needs to be captivating. Lead with a promise, surprise your readers, and they will read the whole thing.
- **The last tweet is the launchpad.** Here, add any links or call-to-action items that you want a reader who enjoyed your piece to act on. Consider that if someone just read your 20-tweet behemoth, they loaded up on a lot of value and might be ready to reciprocate right there and then. Allow them to do so. Ask them to visit your blog, sign up for your email list, or check out your eBook there.
- **Create a noticeable pace** between those two tweets. Keep readers engaged, either through suspense or — better yet — consistently high quality.
- **You can easily resurrect threads by adding more tweets to them.** I did that quite successfully with my *Zero to Sold book launch thread.* For many months, I added sales figure tweets and screenshots, constantly bringing the thread back onto people's timelines.
- **One idea per tweet.** This keeps the whole thread more readable and also allows for individual tweets to be quoted and shared.

Threads are particularly useful for these kinds of content:

- step-by-step tutorials
- longer suspenseful narratives like a particular experience, journey, or situation
- a list of best practices you have learned

Adding numbers (like KP is doing in the thread above) is optional. While it's useful to know how many more tweets are coming, people will only continue reading if the content is engaging. Focus on making every single tweet so good that your followers want to read the next one.

There is another very attractive kind of thread: the curated thread. This kind of long-form tweet is less of an essay and more of a magazine article with many visual components. Consisting of many posts of pictures or links', this curated thread is a collection of resources and narratives that often encourage the reader to chase interesting content to other blogs and websites.

Here is an example by Sunil Kumar, sharing his learnings from the course purchases he made in a year:

Sunil Kumar
@sunilc_
...

I bought a lot of courses in 2020 to improve many of my skills:

- development
- online presence
- content writing
- AWS
- mindset
- freelancing
- marketing

These were the best investments I made during the year.

Links: 📕

2:25 PM · Jan 5, 2021 · Twitter Web App

166 Retweets **8** Quote Tweets **631** Likes

Sunil Kumar @sunilc_ · Jan 5
Replying to @sunilc_
1. Everyone Can Build a Twitter Audience:

by @dvassallo

EVERYONE CAN BUILD A TWITTER AUDIENCE

Everyone Can Build a Twitter Audience
Over the past 14 months, my Twitter account has grown from 150 to 24,000 followers (now 60,000+). How did I do it?First, the backstory...
🔗 gumroad.com

♡ 2   ↻ 3   ♡ 40

Sunil Kumar @sunilc_ · Jan 5
2. Standing Out in 2020: Doing Content Right:

by @stephsmithio

Standing Out in 2021: Doing Content Right
Currently sold: 2800+ copiesThe Internet has created an age of infinite leverage. Anyone can reach thousands (if not millions) of ...
🔗 gumroad.com

♡ 3   ↻ 2   ♡ 26

Sunil Kumar @sunilc_ · Jan 5
3. The Complete Freelancing Bundle:

217

In his first tweet, Sunil sets up the expectation for a long list of links and insights. He promises to list only the best, which is vague enough to kindle the interest of those people that only find a few of the topics he hints at interesting.

In his final tweet, he also asks for people to retweet it to reach more people. While begging for followers is usually frowned upon, asking for a retweet is a common practice. Ask, and you shall receive.

When you write curated threads, try not to overwhelm people with options. There are thousands of interesting links you could share, but a reader's cognitive capacity sharply declines after a few interesting resources. You don't want to lose your reader mid-thread, so keep it manageable. Compared to insight threads, there often isn't a buildup of suspense because there is no narrative structure. You can remedy this by interjecting a few tweets between resources in which you build up such a story: share your thoughts on the links in the thread right before or after the tweet that contains the link.

The Quote

Another winning way of creating content is to share a quote. This can be considered curated insight from outside the social media platform on which you operate. Here is Ryan Holiday sharing a Pirsig quote:

Ryan Holiday ✔
@RyanHoliday

"Art is anything you can do well. Anything you can do with Quality." Robert M. Pirsig

9:30 PM · Oct 1, 2020 · Hootsuite Inc.

61 Retweets   **4** Quote Tweets   **370** Likes

It's short, it's impactful, and Ryan receives the full engagement for something someone else wrote. Attribution is the one thing that every quote should have. If you act like the insight is yours, someone will point it out, and you will be in trouble. If you make it very clear that you are quoting, people will appreciate this, as this allows them to learn more about the original author of the quote as well.

You can also share your thoughts on the quote, but I recommend doing this in reply to the tweet. A standalone quote is often compelling and will cause people to share it because of the clarity and brevity it represents.

The Observation

This is the on-platform version of a quote: directly quote-tweeting an insight with commentary.

It's a value double pack: not only do your followers get to see the insightful content by the person you are retweeting, but they also gain value from your insightful commentary.

That means that you will need to have something meaningful to add. The bare minimum is an acknowledgment of the value of the statement you're quoting, as Cam Thomas is doing here:

Cam Thomas 🇺🇸
@MadWickedCam

I've worked for five certifiable millionaires in my lifetime.

None of them had degrees or professional certifications.

> **Lawrence King** @lawrencekingyo · 11h
> The most successful people I know are usually self-educated

12:15 PM · Apr 30, 2021 · Twitter for iPhone

In his quote tweet, Cam condenses his experiences with wealthy people into a single powerful statement. Short, itself very quotable, and to the point.

Here is Jimmy Daly, highlighting a particular reply by Fadeke Adegbuyi:

Jimmy Daly
@jimmy_daly   ...

this is very good advice for folks early in their careers. and
it's probably great advice later in your career too, esp if
you end doing something that you don't love.

> **Fadeke Adegbuyi** @fadeke_adegbuyi · Jan 28
> Replying to @huntermoonshot
> Try on different marketing hats and see what sticks!
>
> Joining an early-stage startup as a marketer is a quick education on what you
> would like to focus on. You're doing a bit of everything –– PR, copywriting,
> social, ads, emails, blogging, growth experiments, partnerships, etc.

12:26 AM · Jan 29, 2021 · Twitter Web App

1 Retweet   **13** Likes

Contextualizing another person's tweet is a way to add
value, too. It invites engagement and shows that you don't just
have an opinion, but you have the experience to back it up. This
is generally a good idea for content: providing context for
information in a sea of isolated voices. Doing this will help your
community a lot, and it will show how concerned you are with
making it a better and more cohesive place for people to
interact.

The Question

While teaching people by sharing unique insights and resources
is a great way to establish your personal brand as a domain
expert, you can always create an opportunity for people to learn
from each other. Asking a question starts such a conversation,

as inviting your followers to share their knowledge can create amazing learning experiences.

This simple question about music preferences while building software netted Maxi Contieri, a software engineer, a lot of engagement. Hundreds of people replied, and an animated discussion about the benefits of certain kinds of music ensued. Friendships were forged, playlist links were exchanged, and scholarly debates were held about how music impacts our code quality, all from one question.

If you want to create content with a question, consider this:

- **Specific questions will result in reduced engagement but likely higher-quality answers.** If you ask a question that only an expert can answer, the number of people who will engage directly with the post will be lower, but the results will be remarkable once they do. Wording a question in such a way that experts can't resist replying is a skill you will develop over time. Just keep asking.

- If you are **looking for a general response**, make sure that you **ask a general question**.
- **Make your question specific by giving people an idea of what answers you're expecting.** *"What tactics do you use to increase your email signup conversion rate?"* is much clearer than *"How do you get more followers?"*

Here are specific kinds of replies to ask for:

- Tactical advice about professional topics: *"How do you make sure you always send your freelancing invoices on time?"*
- Anecdotes that someone has for a particular issue: *"Have you ever offered a yearly plan in your SaaS? How did that go?"*
- Recommendations: *"What tools do you use to edit your podcast episodes?"*
- Alternatives: *"Besides using Google Sheets, how can I best keep track of my stock market investments?"*
- Decisions: *"Is it a good idea to learn Python if I want to go into Machine Learning?"*
- Resources: *"I can't seem to find a good guide on audience-building. Any idea if someone is writing a book on that issue?"*
- People to follow: *"I've just joined the Marketing Twitter community. Who should I follow?"*
- Opinions: *"What do you think of the problems with privacy in advertising?"* — but be careful with those questions. They can often invite controversy and heavily polarized conversations that you might not want to have your name attached to.

Questions are best used in conjunction with other types of

content. A question plus an infographic and a quick how-to tutorial can serve as a content base for you to build a thread around. You can also use questions within longer threads by including a *"How do you feel about this?"* tweet at the end that invites reader comments and engagement.

A question invites responses. A statement invites a nod. That might sound like the more you ask, the more engagement you will get. But that's a false assumption. You want a balance here. Just asking questions all the time makes your account less interesting to follow. It's the same for just posting quotes or just posting visuals: people want variety. As a well-rounded person, your content should be equally varied.

The Link

Most social media platforms try to keep their users engaged within the platform. That also means that anything that might cause a user to go somewhere else could be considered adversarial content. This seems to be the case on LinkedIn in particular, where the activity-feed algorithms penalize posts with external links. Luckily, Twitter is the perfect place to post external links — even though there is some debate about whether it should be done in the first tweet or in a reply. I prefer to risk a small penalty to my reach if a link increases the potential engagement with the tweet, in any case.

Tweets that include links are most often used to get people into external funnels: here is Alex Llull sharing a blog post he wrote. He hints at the contents of the post, makes it sound exciting to read, and then adds the link to his personal blog, where people can read the whole post and learn about the professional services he has to offer.

Alex Llull
@AlexLlullTW

Sometimes, when I finish my workday, I find this little monster inside my head that yells "It's not enough!".

This is how I plan to fight back. A post on being "always ON" as a creator.

Got a bit darker than usual, would love to hear your thoughts!

The Creators' Curse
Sometimes, when I finish my workday I find this little monster inside my head that yells "It's not enough!". This is how I plan to fight back.
🔗 alexllull.com

12:56 PM · Jan 28, 2021 · Twitter Web App

6 Retweets **34** Likes

Alex Llull @AlexLlullTW · Jan 28
Replying to @AlexLlullTW
Reading time under 3 minutes!

♡ 4

While this might seem self-promotional, it only is to a certain degree. The blog post invites community discussion and

225

is not aimed at selling anything. In fact, Alex's writing shows how much he cares about the community he's in, and sharing the post with its members will elevate him as both an expert and a community enabler.

But you don't just have to share your off-platform content. Any informative and interesting discoveries from the web will do. Here's a particularly well-performing link tweet of mine:

Arvid Kahl
@arvidkahl

Genius. They wrote a script to make a PDF look like it's printed, signed, and then scanned again. Because digital signatures are still not accepted in many places while a signed and scanned printout is.

This is hacking bureaucracy. I love it!

Edouard Klein / falsisign
For bureaucratic reasons, a colleague of mine had to print, sign, scan and send by email a high number of pages. To ...
🔗 gitlab.com

10:08 AM · Apr 10, 2020 · Twitter Web App

2,541 Retweets   **233** Quote Tweets   **6,839** Likes

I remember how this one happened. I found this link being discussed on a developer forum and quickly tweeted it out with a short description. The software engineers in my audience picked it up, and it went slightly "viral."

I don't believe you can magically conjure up viral tweets. Who picks up your tweets is the one thing you can't ever control. You can increase the opportunity surface by sharing interesting things first and in an easily shareable form, though.

When you share links, make sure you include the following in your tweet:

- **A summary** of what the reader can expect to find — and why that is interesting.
- **A warning** about potentially annoying parts of the linked resource: **paywalls, popups, trackers.**
- **Attribution** to where you found the link if that is in the interest of that party. It's never wrong to give credit when you operate under the abundance mindset.
- If needed, an indication that the resource you share might **not be safe for work.**
- An indication of **reading time** if it exceeds a few minutes. If you're sharing a long article, give people the chance to save it for later when they have time.
- **Link directly** to the resource you want to talk about. Don't make people sign up for stuff or go through a 10-step ordeal to get to what you want them to see.

You won't be able to build an audience on links alone, but they can be a valuable in-between kind of content. I recommend saving any interesting link you come across in a spreadsheet or something like a Notion table. When the time comes to share something with your audience, you'll have a reservoir of thought-provoking links at the ready.

The most important thing is that your links are useful. No matter if they are pointing to your own off-platform content or someone else's work, consider that they have to be valuable to your audience. If someone clicks your link and feels you wasted their time, they will tell you — and everyone watching — in public. If you wonder if any given link is worth posting or not, it probably isn't.

The Progress Update

Let's get a bit more personal. So far, I have introduced a lot of content that can be considered "evergreen." A good quote or a link to a timeless resource can be posted at any point and get some good engagement. But that makes them quite interchangeable. If you want to create content that is uniquely yours, consider sharing what you are working on, what you're learning, and where you're struggling.

This is very easy when you commit to building in public. You'll want to post about your progress regularly, and a progress update will come naturally. Check out this update by Matthias Bohlen of Get The Audience:

Matthias from Get The Audience ···
@GetTheAudience

Stats at the end of day #89, building GTA #buildInPublic:

- 53 users on GTA, 2 paying, 5(!) trialing
- 103 (+7) audiences
- 98142 (+11158) tweets imported
- 73326 (+8827) tweeps imported
- 399 (+44!) twitter followers

12:06 AM · Jan 23, 2021 · Twitter Web App

1 Like

♡   ⟲   ♡   ↑

Marco Spörl @MarcoSpoerl · Jan 23 ···
Replying to @GetTheAudience
It's kind of mesmerizing to read these stats every day. Thanks for sharing
and congrats on today's success!

♡ 1   ⟲ 1   ♡ 1   ↑

Matthias from Get The Audience @GetTheAudience · Jan 23 ···
Thank you Marco for your kind words. This encourages me to go on with
#buildinpublic !

♡   ⟲   ♡ 1   ↑

Matthias keeps a daily tally of the primary metrics of his
product and the business. You can see pretty clearly from the
response to this particular update that people are interested in
seeing such data appearing on their feeds on a regular basis.

An update can be a lot of things:

- a milestone reached
- a celebration of a particular success
- an explanation of a particular choice and its impact
- a failure and how it happened
- a strategic shift in how you approach your business

- a shower thought that led you to create a particular feature or piece of content

If you had a big announcement post about your intention to build in public, you can always attach or share your progress update tweet within that thread. This will keep people informed of your current activities and the context in which they are undertaken.

The Visualization

How about we explore another medium? Instead of conveying your insight with text, you try to add value with visualization?

Here is Craig Burgess, an experienced designer and a visual communication expert, talking about clarity — and visualizing it in an immediately accessible way.

Craig is trying to finish The Magic Visual
@craigburgess

Replying to @craigburgess

The higher purpose of all design is to communicate an idea.

Remove anything that doesn't serve that higher purpose.

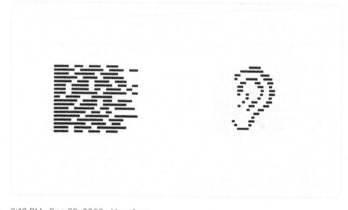

3:10 PM · Dec 29, 2020 · Hypefury

2 Retweets   **16** Likes

The wonderful thing about tweet-sized insights is that they lend themselves to visual reinterpretation. Visualizing value — also the name of a popular visual design and entrepreneurship course — is a great way to share insights that capture people's attention. After all, Twitter users see text tweets all day, and it takes a while for our brain to parse and understand the text. An image, however, is almost immediately understood and will cause us to stop and engage. Visual content is quite literally eye-catching.

Visualizing someone else's insight is a veritable way of adding value to your community's ongoing conversations. Some people may not have truly understood a concept until they see it visualized. The effort you put into learning how to make visualizations will be absolutely worth it and show progress right here in your audience-building results as well as your marketing and sales approaches with your business.

Reframing ideas isn't limited to iconographic simplification, however. The spectrum of visual media is huge, and since everyone learns things in different ways, many visual explanation approaches have a place on Twitter.

Alex Paval took a blog post I wrote and created a stunning mind-map.

Alex Paval
@lexpaval

🚀 There are multiple ways to grow on Twitter, but my favorite way to do that is the @arvidkahl way.

🎆 Being an engagement king has its pros and cons.

🌐 Here is a mind-map of how he does it.

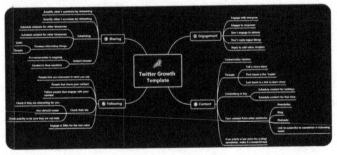

2:11 PM · Jan 27, 2021 · Twitter Web App

59 Retweets **22** Quote Tweets **378** Likes

As it happens, Alex has been making mind-maps for many years but never shared them with anyone, thinking they were nothing special. It turns out that people love them, and Alex has found his niche as a prolific mind-mapper. This is using your unfair advantage to build a personal brand.

Here are a few ideas and concepts to explore:

- Create line and bar charts to visualize time series.
- Show decision trees and flow charts to explain a complicated logical process.
- Visualize dependencies and connections in Venn diagrams and network graphs.
- Use visual metaphors and iconography.

I really recommend learning more about visual communication. While not everyone is a designer, we can all benefit from expressing our knowledge in a multitude of ways.

The Shoutout

So far, we have looked at insights and how we can communicate them to our audience. This is the engagement-focused side of content creation. But there is an empowerment-focused side as well, and that one can be equally useful for building an audience.

Instead of talking about a particular insight, how about you talk about someone in your community? Let's look at Atray Agrawal, giving Janel a well-deserved shoutout for being an inspirational founder.

Atray Agrawal
@atrayagrawal

@JanelSGM is one of my favorites on twitter. Her journey is inspiring.

She's a great example of new creators in the Passion Economy. A big proponent of Build in Public.

And I believe Build in Public is the Bedrock of Passion Economy.

Here's why:

> **Janel** @JanelSGM · Oct 13, 2020
>
> I used to lurk on Twitter, admiring the work and words of others.
>
> Ever since I started writing & sharing my thoughts online, I've gotten to know some of my heroes.
>
> Stop lurking. Start sharing.
>
> What's obvious to you might be insightful to others.

6:39 PM · Nov 17, 2020 · Twitter Web App

3 Likes

A shoutout tweet can be a quote tweet, a thread, or anything else. It's not the form but the intention that makes it a shoutout: the goal is to highlight a fellow community member for their contributions. You can expose your audience to a new and interesting person to follow, enabling your audience to check out their work and see how much they're contributing to making the community a better place to be.

This reputational gain will always — in part — come back to you. By connecting your audience with people from whom they can learn, you become an integral part of their journey. This is an act of connection and kindness that people won't forget.

The person who will remember it the most is the person you gave the shoutout to. No matter if you introduce them to an audience of a few dozen people or several thousand, you're giving them something incredibly meaningful: belief capital. They will feel that you trust them and their work enough to expose them to a bigger audience. Since trust is hard to earn, they will understand your shoutout as something uniquely meaningful.

Shouting out a person on a public platform is a surefire way to increase their opportunity surface. I have seen this over and over again: a person gets introduced to a new audience, and someone from within that new audience creates an opportunity for them: a sale, a partnership, or a new project. With a single tweet, a new path emerged, and a new adventure began. Can you imagine any better way to add value to someone's entrepreneurial journey than to gift them with more opportunities?

It is great to let other authors know that you enjoyed their work. This will encourage them to deliver their content regularly, and it'll give them public recognition for what they already have created and shared. No matter if people are already big shots in their industries or underdogs setting out on their journey, I love to celebrate others for what they create.

There is a variant of the shoutout: introducing a new member to the community. This is particularly powerful once you have already built a sizable audience for yourself. You'll be able to get someone started without having to painfully find their first few followers, and you can be very sure they'll remember this act forever.

You're also allowed to shout out people who shouted you out. Social proof is not just testimonials: it's about people talking about you and your work organically. Pointing this out to your community is a viable way of leveraging social proof in the wild for your personal brand-building benefits.

This is also true for "earned media" outside of Twitter: any interview, reporting, and articles written about you and your work. Your followers love to see you being celebrated outside of your community, as it both elevates you and reassures them of your expertise and importance. They'll gladly share outside perspectives, both within your community and beyond.

The Follower List

You can shout out people at scale, too. Starting a conversation about the best accounts to follow in your niche is a great way of creating engaging content, as it usually invites responses with further recommendations, just like for Fran Cresswell's list of sustainable living accounts:

Fran does something extraordinarily well: she invites her

audience to recommend further accounts. This ask invites engagement and allows people to share their own lists that they might otherwise keep to themselves.

People love being on shoutout lists. It's a status gain, reputation by proximity with other important names on that list, and creates the general feeling of being seen.

While this kind of content is wonderful for the community, it also will be extremely useful for your audience-building activities: the accounts that others recommend are likely highly active contributors to the community. Following them and building relationships with those influential people will further accelerate your growth as an expert and a connector within your community.

Don't overuse this particular kind of content. If all you post is lists of other accounts, how meaningful is your overall contribution? Lists alone won't build your brand.

The Report

After looking at insights and people, let's take a look at events. Many exciting things happen in any community. Conferences, expert panels, meetups, or webinars all attract experts and learners alike. Sharing your takeaways from such events is very engaging content: you're creating a permanent record of learning from a one-time event that — mainly if it wasn't recorded in full — won't ever happen the same way again.

After taking part in an Interintellect Salon, Mind Apivessa shared her learnings, accompanied by thoughtful visualizations, in a thread:

mindapi
@mindapi_

Education is a meaty space. Any meaningful changes in the space require close collaboration between different stakeholders.

At an @interintellect_ salon this weekend, @katrinadlc and I brought together diverse minds to examine education.

Here are my takeaways

2:34 AM · Dec 21, 2020 · Twitter Web App

2 Retweets   **5** Quote Tweets   **42** Likes

Besides the inviting graphic, the thread itself contains a tremendous amount of insight into the event: what questions were asked, what answers were found, and how it all fits together.

There are a few things about sharing event reports:

- They create a **condensed record of the event** with all the major learnings.
- They allow for new and curious community members to find the **motivation to join the next event**.
- They can **connect the people** who were guests at the event with the larger community.
- They put the event on the map for **potential guest speakers** looking for opportunities.

If you're a regular at a meetup or another recurring event, you can consider creating this content on a regular basis. As the archivist of such events, you will gain recognition within both the in-group and the larger community for bridging the presence gap for those who couldn't attend.

The Poll

People love to vote for stuff. They also love seeing how other people vote for stuff. A Twitter poll is a great tool to get massive engagement from your audience. While it's running, it keeps people excited about the potential outcome. After it's done, it can create a whole new discussion about the data points that can be inferred from the poll outcome.

When Bruno Raljic asked his audience about their link-clicking behavior, he only offered the binary choice of Yes or No:

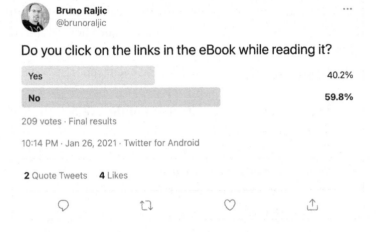

The great thing about such polls is that people who are interested in seeing the results are forced to vote. Unless you present a "View Results" option, voting is the only way to see the current results before the poll is over. I don't recommend adding such an option. Engagement is higher and more honest if the options are all meaningful.

What works to spark further debate is adding something along the lines of "*If you don't find an answer that works for you, please reply and tell me more about it*" to encourage further discussion. While polls are really good at capturing quantitative information, you won't be able to learn more about qualitative problems unless you get people to share them as responses.

The Meme

Posting memes can be hilarious. While it depends on your niche's affinity for less-than-serious content, it usually is a great way to break the ice for conversations about complicated or polarizing topics. But most of the time, it's just plain fun:

UX & Bootstrap
@3rdwave_themes

😄 Designer-developer collaboration in 6 memes
bit.ly/2RMVbsO

#design #development #coding #UI #UX #startup

9:34 PM · Feb 27, 2019 · Buffer

2 Likes

Personally, I consider posting memes to be a rarely optimal content choice. Usually, a good visualization or an in-depth thread will perform better and establish you as more of an expert. But who am I to tell you exactly how hilarious you're allowed to be? Give it a go and see where this leads you.

Flavoring Your Content with Your Personality

We've been talking about niche audiences and communities this whole time. That begs the question of how varied your content should be. If you want to establish yourself as a domain expert in the communities you frequent, then make sure that the over-whelming majority of what you produce is getting you closer to that goal.

But don't become bland. Keep your personality in everything you do. I said this before: if a faceless corporation would share the exact same tweet as you, then you're not putting enough of yourself into your work. Be your honest and truthful self and let it shine in the content you produce.

A funny remark or a story from your personal life here and there is more than welcome in your quest to build a personal brand. There has to be a person to attach the brand to. If you don't come across as a slightly flawed, real human being, people will always wonder what kind of role you're playing. So be yourself and share things about you as a person every now and then.

Consider your content to be the protein in the food, and look at your personality as the seasoning. Without a little splash of yourself, the meal would be bland, and something people would rather forget than remember. Spice it up with the thing that nobody else can do as well as you: being yourself.

Content Alignment and Audience Feedback

Engagement goes both ways. If you are making it hard for people to interact with you and your content, consider adapting to your audience's needs and change what you produce. If the people who'd love to learn from you don't have the time to read your 5,000-word essays, create little summary posts or offer an audio version of your content that people can consume when they walk the dog or drive to work. This is precisely why I started the Bootstrapped Founder podcast after several reading-impaired followers asked me to make my work easier to consume.

Here's a very empathetic example of ensuring that the content fits the audience: Maangchi, a YouTube cooking influencer with a popular channel, noticed that her viewers complained about the portion sizes on her show being too big. Maangchi comes from a big Korean family, where those portions were considered "normal," but she quickly understood that she needed to make portion sizes smaller in her videos for her content to succeed. Her audience loved that.

On Re-Using Content

Creating valuable content is hard. Producing it reliably is even more challenging. Many creators are holding themselves back by believing that they need to create original work at all times. They think that re-using content is a cardinal sin.

I believe differently. There is incredible value in re-using your content.

There is a misunderstanding of what makes content valuable among many people building in public. By focusing only on originality, they miss the equally important but often neglected concepts of accessibility and timing.

If you want your content to have the highest possible

impact, you should give accessibility and timing more consideration.

Content Accessibility

What good is a piece of content if the people it's meant for can't consume it? When I started the Bootstrapped Founder blog, I focused exclusively on written articles. Over time, more and more people flocked to the blog, and the number of people reaching out about alternative formats increased.

Some people don't have the time to read your long-form content because they're juggling their day job, side business efforts, and family life. Others are visually impaired or dyslexic. You can make your content accessible to these potential readers by moving it to another format.

After receiving a handful of those messages, I decided to turn my weekly blog post into a podcast. After writing the article, I record myself reading it aloud. With a short intro and an outro, that's all I need to do to make my writing accessible every week. It may take me about 20 minutes of editing, but it's absolutely worth it.

It doesn't even have to be a different format to be more accessible; it could just be a different distribution channel. Initially, I exclusively wrote blog posts. Now I release my article as a newsletter every week. It's the same text, but it's delivered to my readers instead of them having to visit my blog. The act of creating the newsletter isn't even a five-minute deal: I can use my article verbatim and wrap it into a headline and a few lines of an outro.

The Flywheel Effect

It doesn't even take me 30 minutes to turn my blog posts into a newsletter and a podcast episode each week. From one piece of content spring three distinct pieces with different audiences. This gives me a fantastic opportunity: I can build a flywheel.

Each blog post includes a link to the newsletter signup page and an embedded player for the podcast episode. Every podcast episode links to the blog post in the show notes and also allows people to sign up for the newsletter. Every newsletter episode has a link to the podcast episode and the blog.

Cross-linking your content variations will do a few things:

- **It allows people who have different preferences to find alternative, more easily consumed versions of your work.** Providing options increases your conversion. It also makes your content innately shareable in a medium that the consumer prefers.
- **It diversifies and cements your audience.** The more people you can get to join your owned audience (such as an email list), the better. If you write on a platform like Medium or Twitter, where a company has full control over your account and visibility, allowing people to connect with you directly is critical.
- **It gains noticeable SEO benefits** from having links to your projects on high-authority websites such as podcast-hosting platforms. The more search engines know about the connectedness of your content, the easier it will be for those looking for it to find it.

Good content is accessible. Now that we've figured out the "how," let's look into the "when."

Content Timing

Where a lack of accessibility makes content hard to consume due to certain limitations, being exposed to the right content at the wrong time is similarly problematic. Imagine you write an in-depth article about how to publish a book, but the person reading it hasn't even written the first line of their manuscript yet. They'll need the insight from your work eventually, just not now.

Everyone is at a different stage of their journey. Whatever you create will resonate more strongly with some than with others. But that's not a quality problem or one of not being original enough. The problem is that you "spoke too soon."

The problem of not being able to time the release of your content perfectly for everyone has an easy solution: repeat yourself. When you write content that works best for any particular stage of the professional journey, post the piece of content again a few months later.

The risk of sharing your work over and over is that you reach a point of saturation. Some people who have advanced past a certain level of skill might feel like you're not talking to them anymore.

I saw this happen to an established software engineer. Florin Pop, a developer, teaching other developers how to make money from their craft, pondered publicly if Tech Twitter is dying[3] after seeing a drop in activity and engagement with his sizable Twitter audience. I believe he is witnessing what can be called "Audience Graduation," the process of his initial audience outgrowing the content he produces. Once you have taught everything you know, and your audience has absorbed it, you either need to find a fresh audience or change to cater to your existing audience's new needs.

While this is a long-term problem, you'll need to keep this in mind when picking the themes and topics for your work. Audience Graduation is a "champagne problem": you'll be glad to have it because it indicates that you have succeeded in building a sizable audience. It's a problem nonetheless, and you should prepare for it.

Curation: Re-Using Other People's Content

So far, we have only talked about your own written content. But there is so much more. Originality isn't limited to creating something from nothing. You can also use other people's content in an original way. Here are a few ways of adding value to someone else's work:

- **Contextualization.** Let's take Florin's tweet about his engagement problem. You can share it with commentary, adding your opinion on why he's experiencing this issue, pulling in similar tweets by other accounts, or linking to an article that deals with shifting audiences. You enrich the content with your own thoughts and insights, thus creating original content. Debunking an article can work the same way.
- **Summarization.** If you read a long-form article in an online magazine, chances are you can distill it into a list of a dozen insights. That list is valuable, allowing interested readers to discern if they should spend half an hour reading the whole thing. You can become a trusted source of condensing knowledge. That much denser information is original content.
- **Recommendation.** With all the social media noise, it's hard to know what to consume and what to skip. Curating interesting resources, either by providing additional context or a quick summary, can be a viable way of creating content for your audience. You can even turn this into an info product eventually.

As long as you add value, it's perfectly fine to use other people's work.

Re-Using Content Involving You

Finally, there is an interesting in-between type of content that you can leverage: content with and about you, created by others. Be it a shoutout on Twitter, a short interview on a blog, or a fully-fledged podcast episode, anything that involves you will undoubtedly be attractive to your audience.

I have a list of all the podcast episodes I ever appeared in[4] on my blog. Whenever a new one comes out, I heavily feature it on my social stream and add it to the list. Provided that the host agrees, I can even rebroadcast the episodes on my own show. This is advertising for the other podcast, and it brings some diversity to my show.

In the same vein, I have turned a lot of conversations on Twitter into articles and podcast episodes. Often, those conversations sparked a certain topic to stay on my mind for a few days to finally result in an essay on the issue. In the same flywheel-like way, this results in three pieces of content that spark further discussions on the subject, which leads to more ideas for content.

Creating original content is great, but it's not the only way to provide value to your audience. By allowing for accessibility, understanding that different people need to learn about things at different times, and re-using content made by other creators, you can generate immense value for those who are listening to you.

Don't Drown Other Voices with Too Much Content

You can definitely overdo it with content, no matter how valuable it is. If a person follows a hundred people on Twitter but every second post on their timeline is from you, they are very likely going to unfollow you as you're drowning out the other voices. The abundance mindset goes only so far with most people. The moment your content is working against your followers' best interest — to learn many things from many people — you're not providing value anymore.

That's why you should investigate the average amount of tweets that people in your community publish on any given day. Best do this before you start your serious audience-building efforts. The goal is to prevent your audience from feeling suffocated by your onslaught of insights. If you want to build a long-term relationship based on trust and curiosity, you'll need to set up a schedule.

SETTING UP A TWITTER ENGAGEMENT, EMPOWERMENT, AND CONTENT SCHEDULE

I have found that my audience-building process is much more structured with a schedule: the inputs are clear, and the outputs are measurable. It allows me to automate large parts of my Twitter engagement while also allowing me to actively build relationships with people in the community.

Before we dive into the details of a schedule, you need to consider two important factors that apply to every single audience out there: local distribution and global distribution.

Local distribution is an attention problem. Your workday only has so many hours, and you can't spend them all on Twitter. How can you make sure that you find enough time to build meaningful connections with those who are using Twitter at the same time as you? How can you make sure you still have time for the work on your business?

Global distribution is mostly a time-zone problem. Where is the majority of your audience located on the planet? When are they most active, and when are they most likely to be on Twitter? How can you make sure you reach as many followers as possible with your Twitter activities?

This is more complicated than it first looks. Many Twitter

guides out there actually claim to be able to tell you the best overall time in the day to tweet. Most often, it's 1:00 pm EST. Can you imagine if this was truly the case and everyone optimized for that? Every single tweet on Earth being sent out at 1:00 pm EST would probably not result in optimal engagement. Additionally, this is very US-centric. And that is gross negligence in a global economy. However, there are data-driven tools[1] being created that find perfect posting times for your specific audience.

Let me share some insights into my personal audience. While the majority of people who read my blog and follow my Twitter shenanigans are from the United States — not surprisingly, as I communicate exclusively in English — I also have large audiences in India, Australia, and Europe. If I only optimized my activity for a US-centric audience, I'd lose out on my Aussie friends and most of my Indian friends as well. Of course, I don't want that, which is why I spread my scheduled Twitter activities over a larger time window that includes at least part of the day for everyone in my audience.

Since I love to sleep and I can't be awake for 20 hours a day, I had to find ways to accomplish my audience-building goals by balancing two activities:

- Automate anything that optimizes your reach.
- Do anything manually that increases your connection.

That means that my Twitter activities have two distinct parts: setting up automation systems and taking the time to connect and interact.

Let's build a schedule to make sure that you can start consistently building an audience.

Arvid's Daily Twitter Schedule

Here are the daily goals I have set up for myself, split into manual and automated tasks:

Manual tasks

- **Every day**, I want to **engage** with at least **three major influential accounts from my community**. That should preferably be a reply to their latest message but can also be an older piece that got a lot of engagement.
- **Every day**, I want to **share** at least **five good fresh tweets** as a simple retweet to boost their initial audience.
- **Every day**, I want to **celebrate** at least **three Twitter users** for something they have recently shared or accomplished as a quote tweet.
- **Every week**, I want to spend an **hour brainstorming new ideas** for valuable content tweets and schedule them for the rest of the week.
- **Whenever I create** some off-platform **content** (like a blog post or podcast episode), I want to **schedule a post** for around the time when that content is released.

Automated tasks

- **Every day**, I want to create at least **one piece of valuable content** as an original post and post it at an optimal point. I want it to **automatically be**

retweeted six hours later so that my followers in other locations get to see it, too.

- **Every day**, I want to **share** at least **10 interesting retweets** at random intervals during my audience's day. These can be recent or old, which doesn't matter as long as they are insightful.
- **Every day**, I want at least **three** of my **best-performing tweets** from the past to be retweeted to expose them to new followers.
- **Whenever my podcast episode gets published, I want it to be automatically shown on Twitter.**

The manual work is not much different from what you already do on Twitter:

- You engage with other people.
- You reply to their tweets.
- You participate in ongoing conversations.

The only difference is that you'll want to take a certain amount of time every day to reach a daily engagement goal.

Automation is an incredibly powerful tool. From the numbers in my schedule, you can see that of the ~20 tweets that I want to publish every day, half are automated. That means that at some point, I schedule them to happen in the future. I am using a Twitter Scheduling tool called Hypefury for that, both for original content, the automatic delayed retweets, and the retweets that I intersperse during the day. For my podcast, I am using Transistor.fm's automatic release tweet feature.

Hypefury has a feature called "Evergreen Tweets" that allows me to have a random high-performer tweet from my past be retweeted at specific times during the day. Let me show you my Hypefury Posting Schedule:

Posting Schedule

| Every day | | | ∨ | at | ◷ 12:30 | Add New Posting Time | or | Add New Evergreen Slot |

Monday	Tuesday	Wednesday	Thursday	Friday	Saturday	Sunday
8:04 AM	8:05 AM	7:56 AM	7:59 AM	7:59 AM	8:16 AM	8:03 AM
9:01 AM	9:04 AM	9:07 AM	8:45 AM	8:57 AM	9:01 AM	8:58 AM
★ 9:28 AM	★ 9:31 AM	★ 9:31 AM	★ 9:24 AM	★ 9:34 AM	★ 9:31 AM	★ 9:27 AM
9:56 AM	9:58 AM	9:54 AM	10:02 AM	10:10 AM	10:01 AM	9:58 AM
10:47 AM	11:01 AM	11:10 AM	11:07 AM	10:58 AM	11:12 AM	11:07 AM
★ 11:52 AM	★ 12:04 PM	★ 12:08 PM	★ 12:07 PM	★ 12:05 PM	★ 12:10 PM	★ 12:05 PM
12:56 PM	1:07 PM	1:05 PM	1:07 PM	1:12 PM	1:08 PM	1:02 PM
2:11 PM	1:42 PM	2:04 PM	2:07 PM	2:09 PM	1:52 PM	1:58 PM
★ 3:03 PM	★ 2:47 PM	★ 3:06 PM	★ 3:05 PM	★ 3:02 PM	★ 2:53 PM	★ 3:05 PM
3:55 PM	3:52 PM	4:08 PM	4:02 PM	3:54 PM	3:53 PM	4:12 PM
5:05 PM	5:01 PM	4:58 PM	4:56 PM	5:01 PM	4:46 PM	4:56 PM
6:56 PM	6:52 PM	6:00 PM	7:02 PM	7:09 PM	7:03 PM	6:56 PM

As long as my queue of content and retweets is filled, something will go out 12 times a day, guaranteed. Even if I don't have any interesting tweets to share, the three daily slots marked with a star will retweet an Evergreen Tweet.

The idea behind this automation is to free up my day. There is no creative difference between retweeting something right now or having a service do that for me six hours from now. There is a significant difference for me to know that while I sleep, a tweet that I selected during my day gets retweeted to an audience on the other side of the globe.

It takes time to find and create meaningful content to fill this schedule. It takes even more time to do all of the creation and curation and wait for the right time to tweet it out manually. If you actually want to work on a business while building an audience, you need automation to assist you.

How to Set Up a Schedule for a Side Project

Now, if you work a full-time job and are building a business on the side, finding over 20 things to share every day is a big ask. It'll be hard enough to find even half an hour a day to work on your side project. Let's look at a reasonable schedule (and a few tips) for a side-hustle that won't demand more than a few minutes each day.

Manual tasks

- **Once a week**, take **15 minutes** to come up with **3–5 tweets and schedule them** on different days, at different times.
- **Once a week**, take another **15 minutes to find 10–20 interesting tweets** from your timeline **and schedule them** between your original content.
- **Every day, retweet** at least **three** interesting articles or insights.
- **Every day, quote tweet one** interesting article or insight with a thought-provoking comment.
- **Once a week** (and whenever you feel inspired), pick one person you admire for their work and give them **a shoutout**.
- Whenever you see someone **struggling or celebrating, retweet their message**.

Automated tasks

- **Automatically retweet** your original tweets six hours after they are published.
- Automatically retweet the 10–20 interesting tweets you have scheduled.
- Once you have a few well-performing tweets, consider setting them to be automatically retweeted at random points.

This approach will give you the chance to batch your preparation work into 30 minutes a week. Even if you don't engage with people on Twitter during the week, these 30 minutes will result in a few dozen engagement opportunities for your audience due to the automation you set up. Whenever you *do* find time to engage with people in real-time, you have a daily goal to reach. Using Twitter intentionally as a tool and not just a place where you hang out and look at memes will significantly impact your personal and professional brand. Use your time wisely.

Of course, you can deviate: this schedule is a framework, not the law. If you see a conversation happening in your community and would rather engage with that than schedule a retweet, go right ahead. This is also part of being your true self. Don't lose your curiosity and unique voice because you have a system in place.

How to Set Up a Schedule for a Full-Time Project

The moment you shift all your attention on a business project, audience-building becomes a more time-consuming endeavor. I recommend taking my personal schedule above and playing around with the numbers and frequencies until you have found something that allows you to work on both your business and your audience at the same time. While you are in the early stages, I would limit the "daily social media time" to a maximum of 30 minutes. While you'll find a lot of value in the community in terms of feedback and encouragement, you need to get other work done, too. Own your time.

TOOLS OF THE TRADE: USING TWITTER PROFESSIONALLY

A great violinist will likely be able to make even a very cheap violin sound good. But give them a Stradivarius, and they'll make it sound mind-blowingly amazing. Professionals do their best work with professional tools.

For your Twitter interactions, the tools that matter can be looked at in two groups:

Operational tools

- **Scheduling tools** like Hypefury are essential. You need to be in control of your time. These tools are your army of robots that will work — and make you money — when you sleep.
- **Monitoring tools** like a well-setup TweetDeck are very helpful. You need to know who interacts with you and what interesting content is being created on your platform.

Research tools

- **Account Analytics** like ilo.so will give you insight into your engagement stats like impressions, follower movement, and which content of yours performs best.
- **Audience Analytics** like Get the Audience and SparkToro will allow you to find out things about your audience in a data-driven way. You'll learn about the best times to publish content, who is influential in your community, and the quality of the followers for any given account.

The one thing you will definitely need is a scheduling tool. From there, explore the other tools to find a mix of software that makes your audience-building journey enjoyable. Just make sure you don't rely exclusively on tools. You'll still need to be able to engage with your audience manually when opportunities come up. Over-automation will make your content predictable and boring.

BUILDING (FOR) AN AUDIENCE

The last few chapters have been heavily focused on building a following around you as a domain expert. Since the Audience-Driven approach is supposed to make you "put your audience first," you need to stay in constant communication with your audience about the way you're solving their problems. Let's look at the other brand, the professional brand you're building: a business that emerges from your work, solving a critical problem that is felt by an existing audience.

Sharing the Journey

If your personal brand is that of a domain expert, then your professional brand needs to consist of two parts: the experienced founder and the successful product. The content you can create for those specific perspectives can overlap with the personal brand work you're doing, but that's not a problem: after all, both brands are connected. I want to highlight a few things that are particularly attractive to your audience when it comes to the professional side of things:

While sharing the founder journey:

- **Share your assumptions and validation strategies.**
  Your prospective customers are very interested to see how in-depth your industry knowledge is. If you are missing something, you'll get feedback on that very quickly.

- **Share your decision-making.** This is itself a validation strategy. If you reason erroneously in public, people will point this out very quickly, and you can both learn and humbly accept the help that they give.
- **Share your failures and struggles.** Honesty is not weakness. Sharing the not-so-perfect details of your journey makes you relatable and humanizes both your business and the people working in it. You can expect a customer who has seen you struggle with your business to think twice before yelling at you in a customer support email.
- **Share "mind level-ups"** — moments when you finally understand something you never understood before. Not only will this increase your professional reputation, it will also teach people at the same time.

While sharing the product journey:

- **Share milestones and metrics regularly.** This serves two purposes. At first, it will show the determination and grit of you as the founder to keep working on your project. It will invite people to support and motivate you. Later, when the numbers are getting more and more impressive, this will work as social proof, further increasing word-of-mouth (due to people syndicating your milestone tweets) and netting you more signups or sales. People love numbers. If possible, share screenshots or structured data that allows people to see progress over time.
- **Share big events in the business, either good or bad.**

Are you working on a partnership? Got the go-ahead to build an integration with a large service? Found a potential co-founder? Share it. Make people feel like they have a stake in the business because they're part of an ongoing story.

- **Share product growth and feature insights.** All things change over time. Be public about how you approach building new features or working on new ideas. Talk about how those features came to be and the process you use to prioritize and validate them. You don't have to spill your secrets to give people a feeling of how you run your business.

Whenever you can, invite people to follow the journey of your business. The more people are along for the ride, the bigger the opportunity surface this creates for you, your business, and eventually your prospective customers.

A Warning About Advertising

When you build an audience, it is understood that you do this for some sort of financial gain. You know it, they know it, and it's perfectly fine. As long as all involved parties come out of every interaction as mutual benefactors, it's a relationship worth having.

Here is how you can forever ruin this relationship: mindlessly advertise to your audience every chance you get.

I am extremely careful when it comes to advertising on social media. I touched on this in the Audience Exploration section of this book: people in communities don't enjoy marketing. They don't want their safe places to be overwhelmed by ads. The moment you join a community, be it on Twitter, Facebook, or anywhere else, you are either with them or you're against them.

Okay, it's not that clear-cut. Not every kind of advertisement will cause you to become a community pariah. There is a kind of marketing that you can do that people usually accept, and that's reciprocation-aware marketing. When you point people to your product or services right after you have provided a sizable amount of value to them for free.

Here is the maximum extent of how I market my book on Twitter:

Arvid Kahl @arvidkahl · Dec 15, 2020 ···
Yesterday's Google outage caused a lot of issues with Login w/ Google, Gmail, admin consoles, and general availability.

Founders, do you reconsider your infrastructure choices after such events? Does this affect your perception of platform and dependency risk?

$\bigcirc$ 16 $\uparrow\downarrow$ 3 $\heartsuit$ 35 $\uparrow$

Arvid Kahl ···
@arvidkahl

Replying to @arvidkahl

I write about this topic in my book as well, particularly about picking reliable tech and building abstractions around it. If you're interested in Zero to Sold, you can find it here:

Zero to Sold — How to Start, Run, and Sell a Bootstrapped Business
Zero to Sold is an actionable guide through all stages of a bootstrapped business: Preparation, Survival, Stability, and Growth. Sold on Amazon and ...
🔗 thebootstrappedfounder.com

7:15 PM · Dec 15, 2020 · Hypefury

7 Likes

$\bigcirc$ $\uparrow\downarrow$ $\heartsuit$ $\uparrow$

Here are a few things that I intentionally do:

- This tweet is a reply to my original tweet that already had some engagement. The marketing tweet is not content by itself; it is contextualized to the valuable content above.
- This tweet isn't trying to sell anything right here. It only offers a link to a landing page. I make sure the preview image shows the product, as this is an opportunity to expose the book cover to my audience.
- The tweet itself is a promise of finding more insights on a specific topic in the book. It's intentionally specific, as a more generic ad will seem dishonest.

I never just ask people to buy my books. While this would very likely produce sales, it's not valuable content for them. It's definitely valuable for me, but I want to avoid this kind of self-ishness that doesn't benefit anyone else. To me, marketing is most effective and least invasive when it happens during active social media engagement.

In terms of frequency, try to keep promotional stuff under 20%. The moment you start having a sizable audience, reduce that frequency. People follow you for the tangible benefits they can get from you. Being constantly reminded that you want to sell them something will put them off. Audience-driven advertising is "show, don't tell": provide so much value with your regular content and engagement that people can't help compensating you eventually.

What If My Audience is Not on Twitter?

So far, we have talked exclusively about Twitter. But what if your prospective customers are not on Twitter?

You can transfer the concepts introduced in the Audience-Building section of this book to almost any other communica-

ARVID KAHL

tions platform. While the specific technology and terms might be different, the idea of Engagement, Empowerment, and Valuable Content will always allow you to build (for) an audience.

If you want to build an audience on another platform, please check out the materials on the Further Reading website I have set up for you.

As an entrepreneur, I recommend building an audience on Twitter among your fellow founders in any case — even if your customers are not there. It might not create sales or give you customer feedback for your product — you will need to accomplish those with the audience you build on the platform where your prospects can be found. But by building a business in public on Twitter, you will have the full support and encouragement of the founder community to tap into. I don't think I would be where I am today without this amazing entrepreneurial community's help and guidance.

Audience-Building beyond Twitter

Focusing on the main social media platform is a great idea to have the highest possible impact with your Engagement, Empowerment, and Valuable Content. But there is a world outside of Twitter, and it's full of opportunities. It won't take long for people to understand that you're an interesting person to collaborate with. Embrace this with open arms and become an interesting person for other people to get to know.

Here are a few opportunities that you should keep an eye open for:

- **Appearing on podcast.** Follow and interact with podcast hosts who have interesting guests on their shows, and tentatively ask what it might take for you to end up on their show.

- **Giving interviews.** Google where the influential accounts that you follow have given interviews and build a relationship with those editors. Interviews are great, as they leave a permanent record of your journey and allow you to show your personality in your responses.
- **Writing guest posts on niche authority blogs.** You'll benefit from their SEO rankings and will get access to an audience that is completely off-Twitter — which is good, as you can learn more about alternative platforms to concentrate your audience-building efforts on.
- **Speaking at events.** No matter if it's a conference with hundreds of attendees, a meetup of a couple of dozen experts, or a workshop for a small group of learners, spend your time talking to people in public. If possible, have them record the event and make that public, too. This is valuable content to share with your audience.

Always drop your social media handle when you do any of these activities. It's all about leaving traces. The more of these things you do, the more people will recognize you on social media.

Ironically, the best way to set up these off-Twitter activities happens through Twitter Direct Messages. You can easily move your relationships that you have built in public into a private conversation.

Twitter is perfect for what I call "lukewarm outreach": sending a DM to a person you have previously only interacted with through public Twitter conversations. You know each other vaguely, you have had a fruitful conversation once or twice, you both know that you exist and work in the same community. If you think this is not enough to warrant a personal relationship, banish that thought immediately. This is more than sufficient to reach out to the person you want to talk to, no matter how many followers they or you might have.

Twitter DMs are the secret ingredient in your domain-expertise-growth recipe. By reaching out to people you previously would have thought unreachable, you'll get to your audience-building milestones much faster. That's why you're here: to build relationships and win-win situations that elevate your personal brand, your professional brand, and the community as well.

Platform Risk and the Three Kinds of Audiences

Now that we are already looking into reaching audiences outside of your main community, it's a good time to talk about platform risk.

Alex Lieberman, CEO of Morning Brew, shared a very insightful concept: the Audience Funnel[1]. There are three tiers to this funnel: rented audiences, owned audiences, and monetized audiences.

When you build an audience on Twitter, you're creating a **rented audience**. The relationships you build might feel like they are yours, but Twitter effectively owns them. If you lose access to your account or Twitter decides to remove it, your audience is gone. You won't be able to recover it without significant work, essentially rebuilding your audience. Since Twitter is so huge, you can reach a lot of people and build relationships quickly. But they will always be one administrative action away from evaporating. No matter if you build an audience on LinkedIn, Facebook, Instagram, or Twitter, your audience will always be borrowed.

Contrast this with **owned audiences**. They are opt-in audiences, where people allow you to contact them directly without the intermediary of a large platform. Think of an email list or a Telegram group: any audience where you are not reliant on a platform to communicate. You can transfer your email list to another email service provider, and you can take the phone numbers of your users to form another group using another tool. This kind of audience is much more committed to you than a rented one: the opt-in process made this a conscious choice, and handing over your personal email is a much bigger deal than following someone on Twitter.

Owned audiences are built on free content, such as free newsletters or podcasts. Purchases are encouraged through advertisements, but members aren't required to make purchases to be part of the audience. That changes once you build a **monetized audience**. This is the audience with the highest intent and commitments, as they are paying to be part of that group. A membership community or a paid newsletter audience fits this profile. You won't be able to start out with such an audience; it is the potential consequence of having built rented and owned audiences before.

Personally, I have both a rented and an owned audience. On Twitter, I have built a large following of people who like what I do. Some of them have signed up for my free newsletter or have given me their email address as part of a book purchase. I don't want to force anyone to convert from borrowed to owned. Still, I talk about my newsletter and invite people to join it under every blog post that I write. This content flywheel keeps attracting people to my newsletter, where I keep them updated about my books and other income-creating means.

I believe that all audience-building efforts should start at the rented audience level. When you start, you need to have reach and discoverability. At a later point, you can try to extract those audience members into owned and monetized audiences, but a substantial rented audience is in itself a valuable asset: word-of-mouth marketing and community feedback will be essential to your business success.

In the end, it matters less what kind of audience you have and more how much impact you have on their lives. The value you create is why people follow you. The more someone benefits from your work, the more they're likely to reciprocate, which in turn allows you to make a living.

AUDIENCE GRADUATION

A third-grade math teacher is particularly good at teaching one specific audience: third-grade math students. Every year, a new group of students appears, and they receive a top-notch math education.

Private math tutors, however, have to teach students of all ages. They have to educate a very diverse group of people, using many different educational approaches to ensure every member of their audience comes out of the experience with improved skills. Tutors often stick with their students for a long time.

The third-grade teacher sees no problem in teaching different kids every year. That's their job. For a private tutor, that looks very different: they'd prefer to have a long-term relationship with all of their students, no matter what grade they're in. One audience is highly fluctuating; the other one is sticky for as long as possible.

When you build an audience, you will run into this phenomenon as well.

Some audiences are more permanent than others. Over time, you will experience churn in your follower numbers: some people just move on. They graduate from you. You've taught them everything you know, and they now need something — and someone — else.

Audience Graduation happens in every audience, to varying degrees. It depends on how transient your audience is — how likely they are to move on — and that has a lot to do with their most immediate goals.

If you build a brand around teaching people how to get their first marketing gig at an agency, you will experience some churn. After all, your audience only needs your input to accomplish their goal, and they will look for other sources of more advanced knowledge soon after. If you help coders find their first freelancing clients, they will quickly develop the skills to locate clients themselves.

These are short-term goals that have a clear accomplishment threshold. You either find a client, or you don't. If your audience consists of people who learn how to do this from you, they will eventually move on. They'll graduate and look for teachers who help them with the new problems they're facing.

Short-term goals will cause short-lived audiences.

Now take a look at Seth Godin's audience. Millions of people — marketers, founders, developers, writers — hang on his every word, often having been followers for decades already. They have wildly different goals and come from equally diverse backgrounds. Why don't they "graduate" from Seth?

It's because Seth moves the needle. Every week, he explores a concept on his podcast that many of his followers might never have thought about before. Every week, he enriches the lives of those who listen with something interesting, meaningful, and novel.

Before this turns into a "be-more-like-Seth" piece, let me make one thing absolutely clear: the world needs all kinds of teachers, and Seth would very likely agree with this, as he has spoken about this at length in his work. If you want to get your foot in the door as a novice marketer, the concepts that Seth talks about won't be immediately helpful, but "Ten Things to Do to Get the Attention of an Agency" will be.

We need both high-school math teachers teaching our kids and math professors solving breakthrough problems. In fact, we need many more high-school teachers than academics, and the same is true for social media audiences. There are many more people out there trying to take their first steps than already established industry experts. And few of those notable experts take the time to educate the novices.

You don't have to make a permanent choice here. Starting out with a transient audience doesn't mean you'll see them graduate from you forever. Every permanent audience was at some point transient, and only hard work and a structured approach can shift an audience from high graduation rates into low ones.

So what can you do to keep your audience retention high and churn low?

Surprisingly, it all starts with accepting that Audience Graduation happens and that it's fine. It's expected — and commendable — that people become better at what they do and look for more.

There are a few ways of dealing with this:

- **Grow with your audience.** Adjust the themes you talk about to the expectations of your followers. Stay ahead of their journey and teach them as you go. Plenty of founders do that on Twitter: they build in public, sharing their journey and learnings, and they grow alongside their followers. That's an intriguing path: you get to grow yourself, and your audience tags along for the ride.
- **Carve out your expert niche and be consistent.** If you can provide novel and interesting content that makes a difference for your audience, people will

stick around. They are essentially subscribers to your knowledge output. Operate on the bleeding edge of your space and attract people who want to stay informed as well.

- **Build an audience funnel.** If you are serving a transient audience, it's clear that people will leave. You'll need to compensate for that by getting new followers coming in. Get your existing followers to share your content with their peers that would benefit from your insights. Focus on finding new and rising accounts on social media that are part of your target audience. Engage with them, attracting their existing audiences of similar people — people that need your knowledge right now. Actively work on finding "fresh" accounts that can fill your funnel. It's fine if some of your followers graduate as long as new ones take their place in your audience.

- **Understand your cohorts.** Any audience will include people at different stages. Try to understand the progression from one cohort to another, investigate what people talk about most in each cohort — and what they stop mentioning, particularly in the later cohorts. This will allow you to adjust your content strategy to their needs and expectations.

- **Look at other influential people and investigate their audience.** With some digging, you will see how their content has changed over time to serve their audience. You can infer a lot from those shifts.

No matter if you have a wildly fluctuating audience or high retention, it's essential to understand who you are talking to. The remedy for any lack of knowledge is to constantly engage with your audience beyond your own content. Join conversations where they happen, participate in them, and take a mental picture of the conversational landscape every time you find yourself in it.

Follow other thinkers in your space and catalog what they talk about. Have genuine conversations with your followers about where they are and where they are going. Instead of trying to cling to them, find out how you can help them get there.

If you approach empowerment that way, an Audience Graduation is an event you can celebrate. Having helped a person so much that they don't need help anymore is one of the best feelings you'll ever have. It is a true reflection of the abundance mindset put into practice.

THE JOURNEY AHEAD

We have come far: from the humble beginnings of finding the people you want to serve to building (for) an audience that you want to engage with and empower. What a journey!

The great part is that this journey never really ends. Even if you build a successful business and sell it for a life-changing amount of money, you won't ever really stop engaging with your audience. They become a part of you just as much as you are a part of the community. Your personal brand as an entrepreneur and empathetic community enabler will be something that opens many doors and builds a lot of bridges. Most importantly, this journey will allow you to meet people that will change your life.

Thank you for reading *The Embedded Entrepreneur*.

NOW WHAT?

Please take a moment to rate and review *The Embedded Entrepreneur* **wherever you bought it.** It really makes a difference, and it would be very helpful to me.

Head over to **embeddedentrepreneur.com** to find many resources and links that will help you continue your journey from here.

Several templates for the spreadsheets, lists, and documents that I introduced in this book can be found in *The Embedded Entrepreneur Toolkit* at **embeddedentrepreneur.com/toolkit.**

I wrote another book, **Zero to Sold**, that will introduce you to all the concepts and strategies that you'll need to take your audience and product discoveries and turn them into a fully-fledged bootstrapped business. You can find that book at **zerotosold.com**.

Consider visiting The Bootstrapped Founder blog at **thebootstrappedfounder.com**, where you can read my past, current, and future articles. You can stay up-to-date on my writing by subscribing to the Bootstrapped Founder Newsletter at **thebootstrappedfounder.com/newsletter**. Finally, I publish new episodes of the Bootstrapped Founder Podcast regularly at **thebootstrappedfounder.com/podcast**

Now that you've finished the book, I would love to hear from you.

Finally, please send any questions, corrections, comments, crushing criticism or words of encouragement to **arvid@ thebootstrappedfounder.com**. Every email is truly appreciated.

NOTES

Introduction

1. You can find the full blog post with the Fathom story here: https://links.embeddedentrepreneur.com/fathom-mockup

The Audience-Driven Movement

1. This is the Tweet by @patrickc: https://links.embeddedentrepreneur.com/stripe-feature-tweet
2. If you want to see an example of this, check out this Reddit post: https://links.embeddedentrepreneur.com/reddit-post-looking-for-market

An Actionable Guide to Finding Your Audience

1. Learn more about the economics of museum shops here: https://links.embeddedentrepreneur.com/museum-shops

Step 1: Awareness — Think of Possible Audiences

1. You can read the blogpost called "Niches are for suckers" by Amy Hoy here: https://links.embeddedentrepreneur.com/amy-hoy-niches-worldviews

Step 3: Opportunity — Find Out If They Have Interesting Problems

1. More at https://links.embeddedentrepreneur.com/slack-communities-1 and https://links.embeddedentrepreneur.com/slack-communities-2
2. For example, the best plumbing books are listed here: https://links.embeddedentrepreneur.com/best-plumbing-books

Step 5: Size — Find Out If This Market Can Sustain a Business

1. I've written about this before at length on my blog: https://links. embeddedentrepreneur.com/market-size

Community Platforms

1. HubSpot wrote a detailed article on this: https://links. embeddedentrepreneur.com/hubspot-twitter-advanced-search
2. Here's a list of a few free ones: https://links.embeddedentrepreneur.com/ buffer-twitter-tools
3. Example for a problem-solution-question: https://links. embeddedentrepreneur.com/tweet-solving-problems
4. Example of a Tweet seeking an expert: https://links. embeddedentrepreneur.com/tweet-seeking-experts
5. Example of a Tweet looking for a crossover: https://links. embeddedentrepreneur.com/tweet-looking-for-crossover
6. Like StorySaver: https://links.embeddedentrepreneur.com/storysaver
7. It's called FindAReddit: https://links. embeddedentrepreneur.com/findareddit

Offline Events during a Global Pandemic

1. Learn more about the Spanish Flu's impact on the world economy here: https://links.embeddedentrepreneur.com/spanish-flu

How to Take Notes in Communities

1. There are certain intricacies to taking and making notes. Read the Ness Labs article here: https://links.embeddedentrepreneur.com/note-taking-to-note-making
2. Like Ness Labs: https://links.embeddedentrepreneur.com/tweet-note-taking-communities

Impostor Syndrome and Building Capital

1. Read more about this particular quote here: https://links. embeddedentrepreneur.com/impostor-syndrome
2. Learn more about this very common trope here: https://links. embeddedentrepreneur.com/heroes-journey

The Practice of Audience-Building

1. Learn more about how to integrate accountability into the Four Tendencies here: https://links.embeddedentrepreneur.com/gretchen-rubin-accountability
2. Like Atomic Habits: https://links.embeddedentrepreneur.com/atomic-habits
3. Being indistractable is taught in Nir Eyal's book: https://links.embeddedentrepreneur.com/indistractable
4. More at https://links.embeddedentrepreneur.com/rule-of-seven
5. Read more on Jakob Greenfield's blog: https://links.embeddedentrepreneur.com/dangers-of-metrics

Engagement

1. I am fascinated by these principles. Learn more about proximity here: https://links.embeddedentrepreneur.com/gestalt
2. I love reading up on logical fallacies. It never hurts to know how your brain tricks you. Learn more here: https://links.embeddedentrepreneur.com/logical-fallacies

Empowerment

1. The concept of "Luck Surface Area" has mind-blowing effects when applied to your life: https://links.embeddedentrepreneur.com/luck-surface-area

Valuable Content

1. This is all about being inclusive: add image descriptions, caption your videos, and more: https://links.embeddedentrepreneur.com/twitter-accessibility
2. Learn more here: https://links.embeddedentrepreneur.com/power-words
3. Find the tweet and replies here: https://links.embeddedentrepreneur.com/is-tech-twitter-dying
4. You can find all my public appearances here: https://links.embeddedentrepreneur.com/about-arvid

Setting up a Twitter Engagement, Empowerment, and Content Schedule

1. Like Chime: https://links.embeddedentrepreneur.com/chime

Building (for) an Audience

1. Find the source tweet for the Audience Funnel here: https://links.embeddedentrepreneur.com/audience-funnel

ACKNOWLEDGMENTS

This book was written in public. I believe that a book about understanding and building audiences should be created with and for an audience. For that reason, I shared the book's progress on Twitter and invited several hundred alpha readers to read through and comment on the first drafts of this book.

And comment they did. I received over 2000 comments, notes, and suggestions from my alpha reader squad. This has been the most social editing experience I have ever taken part in. I am beyond grateful for all the perspectives and insights I have gained from this experience.

My alpha readers turned a rough and uneven first draft into a much more polished and accessible book.

I would like to thank my alpha readers:

- @DanSchoonmaker,
- @KimStacks,
- @MrGregZen,
- @OpsDrill,
- @PaiNishant,

- @_justirma,
- @alsayed87,
- @ayushtweetshere,
- @bartszczepansky,
- @daltondemery,
- @dankremerov,
- @eaplmx,
- @farez,
- @heystefan_,
- @honeydreamss,
- @jmmadruga,
- @joshcirre,
- @justinzack,
- @kasperkamperman,
- @maxuuell,
- @poppacalypse,
- @quesada,
- @thdaraujo,
- @uxdaveh,
- @vikivojcik,
- Adnan A M,
- Akash (@go_relay),
- Albert Wieringa,
- Alperen Belgic,
- Andrew Hodson (@MyBuddyAndrew),
- Andy Janis (@AndyJanis_),
- Arav Narula (@tregsthedev),
- Başak Anil (@basakbuilds),
- Charlie Holtz,
- Daniel Jiang (@ikigaibydesign),
- Daniel Sim (@drsim),
- David Butler,
- Dimitris Karavias,

- Dr. Dominik Dotzauer,
- Dušan Popović,
- Fernando Rivero,
- Gabi Rotaru,
- Germán Martínez,
- Habib Khan,
- Hamid Moosavian (@hmoosavian),
- Harish Garg,
- Ivan Nyagatare,
- Jaime Iniesta,
- Josh M. Newman,
- Khalid Azmi,
- Laszlo Sragner (@xLaszlo),
- Madhuri (@iruhdam24),
- Mathias Michel,
- Matthias Bohlen,
- Michele Hansen,
- Miguel Piedrafita (@m1guelpf),
- Nora Crosthwaite (@NoraCrosthwaite),
- Onur Ozer (@onurozer),
- Oshisanwo Jubril,
- Prathamesh Krisang,
- Richelle Delia (@RThomasPhD),
- Roman Imankulov,
- Sathyanand (@Sathyanand1985),
- Shankar Balachandran (@shan0587),
- Shreya Purohit (@eyeshreya),
- Stephen Moon,
- Sudham Jayanthi (@sudhamjayanthi),
- Tarek Hassan (@devtarek),
- Ujjwal Sukheja,
- Yannick Veys (the co-founder of my favorite Twitter tool Hypefury, @Yannick_Veys)

There were countless other readers who I didn't mention in this list. I am grateful to every single one of you.

Ever since the days of writing Zero to Sold, I've been chatting with Rob Fitzpatrick, author of The Mom Test, The Workshop Survival Guide, and Write Useful Books. Rob has been extremely kind and supportive, helping me on my writing and publishing journey with his insights and anecdotes. Thanks, Rob.

Rob is also the reason I had access to HelpThisBook, the platform I used to gather my alpha reader feedback. Together with Devin Hunt (who is also his co-author on The Workshop Survival Guide), he built this platform for authors like me who wanted to work with their audience to create a better — and more useful — book. Thanks for making that, Rob and Devin.

From there, I took the alpha-reader-approved manuscript and handed it to my trusted editor Joanna Pyke, who did a marvelous job (just like she did with Zero to Sold) to pull it all together and surface the remaining inconsistencies. Thank you again, Joanna.

A big thank you goes out to Yasir Farhan, who designed the cover of this book. An equally huge shoutout goes to Graeme Crawley, who created the beautiful illustrations in this book. Thank you!

The book could not have happened without the loving support of my favorite person, my partner Danielle. Thank you for the countless conversations about the book, its contents, and our shared experiences. Thank you for being my anchor, conscience, inspiration, guide, and inexhaustible well of insight and empathy.

Thank you to everyone who cheered for me when I announced this project. Thanks for supporting me when I felt like working on other things, when I got stuck, and when my vision collided with what my audience expected. This has been an exercise in empathy, collaboration, and relationship-building.

ABOUT THE AUTHOR

Arvid Kahl is a software engineer, entrepreneur, and writer. He co-founded and bootstrapped FeedbackPanda, an online teacher productivity SaaS company, with his partner Danielle Simpson. They sold the business for a life-changing amount of money in 2019, two years after founding the company — a journey that's documented in his first book, Zero to Sold.

He writes on **TheBootstrappedFounder.com** to share his experience with bootstrapping as a desirable, value- and wealth-generating way of running a company.

In the years of running FeedbackPanda (and throughout the many failed attempts before that), Arvid learned how to run a self-funded company. He learned that not every business needs venture capital to succeed, and Arvid claims that most businesses are better off without it.

He wants to encourage other entrepreneurs to see bootstrapping as a viable option.

twitter.com/arvidkahl
goodreads.com/arvidkahl

ALSO BY ARVID KAHL

ARVID KAHL

ZERO TO SOLD

HOW TO **START**, **RUN**, AND **SELL**
A **BOOTSTRAPPED BUSINESS**

Zero to Sold is a comprehensive and actionable guide through
the four stages of a bootstrapped business: Preparation,
Survival, Stability, and Growth.

Find out more at zerotosold.com

Made in the USA
Coppell, TX
08 May 2022

77554150R00174